The Green Witch

Your Complete Guide to
THE NATURAL MAGIC OF HERBS, FLOWERS, ESSENTIAL OILS, AND MORE

ARIN MURPHY-HISCOCK

Adams Media

New York London Toronto Sydney New Delhi

Adams Media
An Imprint of Simon & Schuster, LLC
100 Technology Center Drive
Stoughton, MA 02072

First Adams Media hardcover edition SEPTEMBER 2017

ADAMS MEDIA and colophon are trademarks of Simon and Schuster.

For information about special discounts for bulk purchases, please contact Simon & Schuster Special Sales at 1-866-506-1949 or business@simonandschuster.com.

The Simon & Schuster Speakers Bureau can bring authors to your live event. For more information or to book an event contact the Simon & Schuster Speakers Bureau at 1-866-248-3049 or visit our website at www.simonspeakers.com.

Interior design by Michelle Kelly

Manufactured in China

40 39 38 37 36 35 34 33 32

Library of Congress Cataloging-in-Publication Data
Murphy-Hiscock, Arin, author.
The green witch / Arin Murphy-Hiscock.
Avon, Massachusetts: Adams Media, 2017.
Includes index.
LCCN 2017020010 (print) | LCCN 2017027766 (ebook) | ISBN 9781507204719 (hc) | ISBN 9781507204726 (ebook)
LCSH: Witchcraft. | Nature--Miscellanea.
LCC BF1566 (ebook) | LCC BF1566 .M788 2017 (print) | DDC 133.4/3--dc23
LC record available at https://lccn.loc.gov/2017020010

ISBN 978-1-5072-0471-9
ISBN 978-1-5072-0472-6 (ebook)

Contains material adapted from the following title published by Adams Media, an Imprint of Simon & Schuster, LLC: The Way of the Green Witch by Arin Murphy-Hiscock, copyright © 2006, ISBN 978-1-59337-500-3.

Dedication

For Saya and Sydney, who may be among the next generation of green witches.

Acknowledgments

I would like to thank Eileen and Brett for all their hard work on the new version of this book; I think it's better than ever. Thanks also go out again to the original team at Provenance Press who initially helped me develop and shape this material twelve years ago, especially Andrea. And finally, thank you to all the readers who sent me enthusiastic responses to *The Way of the Green Witch* over the years, and asked for it to be made available again.

Contents

Chapter 6
Keep a Green Witch Garden / 134

Chapter 7
Create and Craft Green Witch Magic / 148

Chapter 8
Become a Natural Healer / 185

Chapter 9
Green Witch Kitchen Recipes / 204

Appendix
The Magical Associations of Natural Items / 233

Introduction

Whatever your reasons for seeking balance you'll find that harmonizing yourself with the energy of nature can help you break free from the stressors in your life and focus on the here and now. And there is no better way to explore the bounty of nature than by following the path of the green witch.

The way of the green witch is the path of the naturalist, the herbalist, and the healer. It is a free-form, flexible, and personalized practice for anyone who wants to explore the gifts of nature and use them to find balance and harmony in life. With *The Green Witch* you'll find the information you need to develop and nurture the spiritual practice of green witchcraft—from advice on walking the green path in the modern world to information on essential herbs, plants, trees, stones, and more. You will find recipes, exercises, ritual suggestions, and directions for making potions and herbal blends for purposes both mundane and magical.

From issues such as the history of the practice to creating your own individual traditions, *The Green Witch* is a positive and practical guide for the modern green witch trying to connect with nature in today's society. What is so relevant and unique about green witchcraft is that it is a highly specialized and solo practice. Not everyone will be drawn to the same things and practice in the same way. It's about finding a workable balance in *your* own life within *your* own setting.

The green witch works closely with nature and its gifts. She uses natural elements to improve the well-being of the physical body, the spirit, and the environment, and works to establish a personal connection with the natural world. It may seem like a challenge to harmonize with nature in today's technological and industrial world. Fortunately, you don't need to remove or reverse modern influences. What you need to do is discover how to connect your modern life to that earlier knowledge that is waiting for you to find it again. The trick is to recognize the presence of green energy in the world today and to see how it still operates.

Listen to the world around you. Open your heart. Rebalance. And enjoy your journey.

Note: Although the green witch and reader are referred to as "she" throughout this text, the path by no means excludes male practitioners, who are more common every day. The pronoun "she" was chosen simply for convenience.

Part 1

Discovering the Green Witch

Chapter 1

What Is Green Witchcraft?

HISTORICALLY, A GREEN WITCH LIVED APART, using the energies of plants and trees around her to heal others. Those who needed her services traveled to see her. These days, a green witch is more likely to be living in the middle of a city or in the suburbs. She could work in any of a variety of fields, such as business, medicine, or teaching, or might be a full-time mom.

A green witch isn't defined by where she lives or what she does to bring home a paycheck. Nor is she limited to working with plants, trees, or herbs. She is not, as people might assume, defined solely by the particular way she expresses her spirituality or by the religion she follows. A green witch is defined by her relationship to the world around her, by her ethics, and by her affinity with the natural world. In essence, she lives the life of a green witch: she lives the green path.

The path of the green witch is an intensely personal path that integrates ability, likes and dislikes, the climate of a particular geographic location, and interaction with the energy of that environment. It isn't a tradition so much as a personal adaptation of an ideal.

The Path of the Green Witch

In popular perception, the practice of green witchcraft is a nature-based expression of spirituality that focuses on the individual's interaction with his or her natural environment. Witchcraft itself is a practice that involves the use of natural energies as an aid to accomplishing a task or reaching a goal. In general, witchcraft acknowledges a god and a goddess (sometimes solely a goddess) and recognizes that magic is a natural phenomenon.

Witchcraft is frequently confused with Wicca, which is a modern, alternative, nature-based religion. While Wicca and witchcraft possess many similarities, including reverence for nature, Wicca is a specific, formal religion. There is a wide variety of forms of witchcraft, with varying degrees of structure. For the sake of this book, the term "witchcraft" refers to the practice of working with natural energies to attain goals, without a specific religious context.

A green witch, then, is someone who lives the green path and is aware of how the energy of nature flows through her life and environment, even if that environment is not the traditional garden and forest setting popularized by fairy tales and romanticized notions.

Why do we use the phrase "living the path" instead of simply saying "practicing green witchcraft"? It's very simple. Green witchcraft is not a practice separate from ordinary life, like ritual magic, for example; it is an all-encompassing, total-immersion experience wherein all of life is a magical experience.

Green witchcraft is not a formal tradition in the sense of Gardnerian Wicca, Dianic Wicca, Feri Tradition, or other established forms. When we use the phrase "the green witch tradition," we do not refer to an unbroken line of initiates or an established body of lore. Instead, we are referring to the various practices from diverse places that come together to inform the modern green witch and wisewoman.

Because the path of the green witch is an individualized solo practice, any modern book on green witchcraft is simply a single author's way of interpreting the practice. Initiation into green witchcraft is technically impossible. There exists no body of formal knowledge passed on through careful training, no established group mind to which you are connected by sacred ceremonies performed by elders. Some modern eclectic groups may base their regular practice on the ideals of green witchcraft, but it's not the same thing.

A practitioner of green witchcraft may pass on her personal knowledge, including her personal notes and writings, to another, but that's not an initiatory process. Reading a specific author's ideas and views concerning the path of the green witch is a form of apprenticeship in which you learn a new way of looking at your world and discover new exercises and techniques that will help you refine and deepen your connection to the natural world around you. This process cannot be as intensely personal as traditional apprenticeship, where the apprentice worked beside the master, but it is a modern form of acquiring the knowledge and skills of one particular practitioner.

THE GREEN WITCH'S OUTLOOK

The concepts of healing, harmony, and balance are all key to the green witch's practice and outlook on life. These concepts embody three distinct focuses:

1. The earth (your local environment, as well as the planet)
2. Humanity (in general, as well as your local community and circles of friends and acquaintances)
3. Yourself

The earth is often singled out as the green witch's main focus, which is slightly unfair. The green witch understands that the earth incorporates the planet and all living things upon it, including animals, plants, and people. In this respect, yes: the earth is a collective term for all living things. However, the green witch also knows that to lump them all together means that we sometimes forget the more individual emphasis each deserves. We can decry the general mistreatment of our planet's water supply, but local action often has more of an immediate effect on our environment than demonstrating in front of an office tower. "Clean up your own backyard" is a phrase the green witch understands well.

People are also the green witch's province. The modern green witch understands that humanity impacts the natural world, not only through how individuals treat it, but also via the energy created by their feelings and beliefs. Just as nature's energy affects us, so too does our energy affect nature, and that effect isn't always positive. Therefore, the green witch seeks to maintain harmony between humanity and nature. She also understands that people affect other people with their energy, and she strives to maintain a harmonious energetic environment in which people can feel calm and empowered to improve themselves in a positive fashion and interact with each other with ease and love.

Finally, the green witch must function in harmony with the realities of her own life. This means working out your own goals and obstacles and knowing your own self so that you can apply your energies and skills to the best of your ability. Your true self is not necessarily the self you wish you could be; it is the self you actually are. Finding this true self can be a remarkably difficult goal. We lie to ourselves on a regular basis, often so well that we are completely deaf to certain aspects of our personalities until the day we die. Working with that shadowed side of ourselves can be rewarding, however, and maintaining a harmony between our darker aspects and our positive aspects brings our personal energy into balance.

ETHICS OF THE GREEN WITCH PATH

In any path related to the expression of spirituality, the concept of ethics is important. Interestingly enough, there are no ethical or moral rules associated with the green witch path other than those that the practitioner already possesses.

Why are there no ethical rules set out in green witchcraft practice? First of all, the practice is so very personal that to create an overarching ethical system would exclude some practitioners or force them to change who they are. Green witchcraft isn't about forcing an individual to change; it's about an individual choosing to harmonize her own life with the energy of nature. Second, the green witch is so in tune with her surroundings that a set of ethical strictures is unnecessary. Knowing yourself to be a part of a greater whole makes it difficult to act against that whole. Working with the earth means that to act against it would be counterproductive, and that includes acting against a member of the earth's extended energy, such as other people, animals, plants, and so forth. It is difficult to act unethically when you understand how everyone and everything is affected by the negativity of such an action.

If you love and respect the world around you, you will not abuse it. The more empathy and sympathy you have for your surroundings, the better you will treat them. This is tied in to the basic Golden Rule found in several religions. It's ethical reciprocity: if you treat those around you with courtesy, they will extend the same to you. What you put out into the world returns to you, and that goes for thoughts, acts, and energy.

With the well-tuned awareness that the green witch strives to possess comes a knowledge of who and what will be affected by her actions and choices. With this understanding, and the sense of responsibility and guardianship for life that she also possesses, a further focus on ethics is unnecessary. Nature is your mother, your father, and your best friend. It makes no sense to harm your kin or friends intentionally. Think of the love and respect you have for the earth. Extend that regard to all the creatures that make up the natural world. Humans, animals, plants, trees—they are all part of nature. Naturally, you treat them with the same respect with which you treat the earth herself.

A Brief History of Green Witchcraft

The practices of the modern green witch have arisen from folk healers and practitioners of folk magic. The modern green witch finds her foremothers and forefathers in village herbalists, midwives, healers, wisewomen, and cunning-folk who performed particular services for their communities.

The duties of these spiritual ancestors of the green witch usually included midwifery and preparation of the dead for burial, as well as the use of various plants to heal mind and body. These people possessed knowledge of both life and death. They knew what kinds of which flora could create both states of existence. These earlier green witches, while often respected, were more often feared or mistrusted because of the knowledge they held. They were often marginalized by their communities and lived alone or away from the social center of the community. Even today, society is often uncomfortable with those who possess knowledge not held by the common man.

It is also likely, however, that the spiritual ancestors of the modern green witch chose to live apart from the center of the community because it is harder to hear what nature has to communicate to you when you are surrounded by people. Being closer to the forests and fields made it easier for the cunning-folk to commune with the energies of the living world of green and to gather what they needed.

Practitioners of folk magic, those who live on the second branch of the green witch's family tree, are not necessarily separate from the first. Sometimes the healers were also spellcasters who performed folk magic particular to the region (such as Pennsylvanian pow-wow), but more often they were just grandmothers who had a talent for "fixing" things. Folk magic is composed of traditions and practices that have been handed down in a geographic or culturally specific area. It generally focuses on divination for love and marriage, agricultural success, and weather prediction.

Owen Davies, author of the fascinating *Cunning-Folk: Popular Magic in English History*, explains that as opposed to being healers, cunning-folk originally dealt mainly with lifting bewitchments from people who believed themselves to be the victims of a curse or of some sort of spell. Witchcraft was the soil in which the careers of the cunning-folk grew; when popular belief in witchcraft ended, the roles of the cunning-folk ended as well.

SIMILAR PATHS

There are other modern paths that resemble the path of the green witch. Kitchen witches and hedge witches observe similar practices, and, indeed, sometimes people use these terms interchangeably with green witchcraft. All three paths have three basic things in common: they are based in folk magic, they do not require a spiritual element, and walkers on all three paths tend to be solitary practitioners.

Before we launch into a full examination of what constitutes the modern green witch's path, let's take a look at kitchen witchery and hedge magic and see how they are similar to and how they differ from one another.

- **Kitchen witches,** who are family oriented, focus on magic performed in the heart of the modern home: the kitchen. The kitchen witch bases her magical practice in her everyday household activities, and cooking, cleaning, baking, and so forth all become the foundation for her magical acts. Sweeping the floor free of dust and dirt may inspire a simultaneous cleansing of negative energy, for example. A kitchen witch works intuitively rather than ritually and may or may not keep track of how she works.

- **Hedge witches,** a term used more in the UK than in the US, live close to nature, often away from urban areas. When you think of the classic wisewoman on the edge of town who was visited for love charms and healing potions, you have a pretty decent idea of what a hedge witch is. The modern hedge witch is usually a solo practitioner of a neopagan path who uses spellcraft as a basis for her work.

Modern practitioners often try to link their practice to some sort of history in order to create a sense of tradition, but that sense of tradition is not as important as the sense of self. This is particularly true of the green witch path.

> It is easy to look back and acknowledge the influences of the past on modern practice, but every green witch creates her own practice. There is no initiation, no adherence to a set of rules. Living the green path is really and truly a reflection of the green witch's inner light.

THE MODERN GREEN WITCH

Despite its so-called progress, our modern society tends to look back to a simpler time, even though pioneer days were probably harder and more isolated than life today. This yearning isn't nostalgia, which is a longing for an airbrushed memory. It is a genuine subconscious draw to knowledge that has been obscured by innovation, progress, and improvement. We don't need to remove or reverse modern innovation and give up our sidewalks and television sets and computers. What we need to do is discover how to connect in our modern environment to that earlier knowledge that is waiting for us to find it again. Removing the technology and replacing it with witchcraft and agriculture-based practice is not the answer. To reverse evolution and merely substitute something older is a denial of the modern world. A green witch does not deny the world around her. She accepts it and seeks to understand how to integrate it into her spiritual practice. The green witch serves as a bridge between past and present, new and old. The trick is to recognize the presence of green energy as it exists in the world today, to learn how to see it as it still operates.

Learning to Identify with the Earth

The main identifying trait of green practice is a close identification with the earth. Although honoring the earth and being aware of the natural world is a large part of the majority of modern alternative spiritualities, the green witch is not necessarily a member of an alternative spiritual path. The main difference between the green path and the neopagan religions is that godforms are not an essential part of a green witch's practice. While the green witch is content to look to mythology and ancient religions in order to deepen personal understanding of how earth energy has been perceived throughout the ages, she does not necessarily worship the gods and goddesses that are expressions and representations of earth patterns and energy. The planet itself is an archetype of nurturing, but further refinement of that archetype is not necessary for the green witch. That being said, a green witch often finds a mythological figure—be it a deity or a hero—who resonates with her personal beliefs and energy. She finds inspiration in this mythological figure. This does not, however, lead to worship of that figure.

Whereas alternative religions promote the idea that humanity is a steward or custodian of the planet, the green witch understands that she is the manifestation of the earth itself, not merely a caretaker. That close sense of identification allows her to work in partnership with the earth's energies.

Someone who honors the earth and considers the natural world her primary teacher is sometimes labeled a nature-worshipper or called a pagan. In modern use, however, the terms are not generally pejorative. They describe people who honor the divine in nature. In New Age spiritual practice, the word "pagan" is being reclaimed by those whose spirits resonate to the heartbeat of the earth itself. So is a green witch a pagan? Many are, but not all. The path of the green witch is not by definition a religious one. It is a spiritual path, yes, but spirituality does not necessarily equate to religion. A green witch can participate in any religion and honor the divine in her own way provided that she still honors nature as sacred and blessed. The green witch sees the divine in all of nature, and each green witch interprets that divinity a little bit differently.

CELEBRATING LIFE

Green witchcraft is an ongoing celebration of life. It is a dialogue with nature, a practice that enriches both the green witch and the earth itself. The exchange of energy produces manifold benefits that may be stated in simple terms: through this dialogue, we heal the earth and the earth heals us. We seek harmony through our actions. We look to balance energies that are askew.

Like other earth-honoring paths, the roots of green witchcraft can be found in the agricultural calendar, seasonal shifts, weather patterns, and folk magic performed for health or fertility. Much of the modern neopagan practice comes from basic green witchcraft practice. Note that the word "roots" is key here: when something is rooted, it springs from a source, but it is still strong and anchored. To deny roots is to deny both foundation and strength. We may see only the trunk and the branches of a tree, but the root system ranges deep and wide.

As green witchcraft is not a formal path, practitioners are free to adapt what they learn to what they need. This doesn't mean merely modifying practices created by someone else; it means adapting yourself to what needs to be done. It means being flexible and responsive to your needs and the needs of the earth.

It's important to note that green witchcraft is not Wicca. Wicca is a formal, structured religion that sets out certain tenets and moral guidelines and whose followers celebrate certain rituals in certain ways. Green witchcraft is a nonstructured, flexible practice that has no set holidays and no compulsory rituals. The green witch is adaptable. She creates her own path according to her individual strengths and talents and the energies and supplies native to her geographical locale.

If you live in Massachusetts, for example, and then move to New Mexico, your practice will shift as you adapt to your new environment, the new flora and fauna around you, and the new energies of the landscape. You yourself will adapt as well. As you settle into a new relationship with the earth as it manifests in New Mexico, you will discover yourself evolving to reflect it in a different fashion than you reflected the environment of Massachusetts.

The Magic of Being a Green Witch

Using the word "witch" invariably brings us to the word "magic." This is a word that can cause confusion. Magic is not illusion, nor is it the artificial manipulation of unnatural forces. In fact, magic is perfectly natural: it is the use of natural energy with conscious intent and awareness to help attain a better understanding of the world around you and to harmonize yourself with the world's energies.

Most green witches find the use of the word "magic" to be irrelevant. Magic implies something out of the ordinary. But to a green witch the mundane is magical. When she senses, responds to, and gently nudges the flows of natural energy around her, nothing could be more natural. She's performing natural magic. Nature itself is magical. The everyday is sacred to the green witch.

Marian Green, the author of *Wild Witchcraft* and follower of a path sympathetic to the green witch philosophy that embraces natural magic and hedge craft, states that, "Magic is the art of learning to recognize these elements of change: the natural patterns of flow and ebb, the times of progress, of standing still and of retreating... Magic teaches us to determine which way the tides of Nature are flowing, to see on which level they run and what they can offer each of us at this moment." In Green's view, magic is learning to harmonize yourself with the forces of nature and understanding how they flow through your life. This is, of course, the life work of the green witch in a nutshell.

Spellcraft is seen as a perfectly natural occurrence along the green path. Is brewing a cup of rosemary tea for a headache a spell? Or is it natural medicine? To the green witch, it doesn't really matter. What does matter is the conscious use of the energies of the rosemary to help heal a temporary imbalance. It is the connection to the natural world and the acknowledgment that we are all a part of that world that allows us to function as a link between the world of people and the world of green.

In short, by opening yourself to the energy of nature, and by accepting that you are a part of that grand symphony of energy and power, you allow yourself to partake of that energy to rebalance your life. Then you can work to rebalance the energies of other situations.

In other witchcraft practices, there are methods by which energy is raised, aimed at a target or goal, and released. The green witch uses energy in a slower, more subtle way. Seeking to be a part of the ebb and flow of the energy around her, she thus does not deliberately collect energy to shape and release. The green witch works from the inside out and moves with the natural flow of the energies instead of seeking to manipulate them.

Using the word "magic" can lead you to view your green witch work as something set apart. In this book, there are no rules for creating a magic circle in which you must work, no compulsory calling on deities, no sequences of formal ritual that must be enacted precisely as written. The practice of the green witch is a fluid, natural, personal practice, one that informs every moment of every day. It is important to recognize each moment as "magical" and full of potential. Everything is magical, in the sense that it is wondrous and unique—every breath, every step, every stir of your soup. Every act is an act of magic. The magic is life itself.

This knowledge must be balanced by the understanding that as a green witch, you carry a sacred responsibility not only to watch over the harmony of your environment, but also to remember that, as author Poppy Palin says in *Craft of the Wild Witch*, "every positive gesture has the potential to become a spell." However, there is a danger in the practice of green witchcraft that familiarity may breed contempt. Recognizing each moment as magical and full of potential, the green witch may end up desensitizing herself to the point where no moment is special. Beware of falling into this rut. Allow yourself to marvel frequently at the joy and power of nature as the seasons cycle through the year, at the beautiful and frightful aspects of sunsets and storms. Every moment is magical because it holds potential, but also because it is merely a moment. The mundane is sacred to the green witch because it is mundane. The word "mundane" itself is derived from the Latin *mundus*, meaning "of the material world," and it is the energy created by the material world that sources the green witch's power.

OATH OF THE GREEN WITCH

Fundamentally, green witchcraft is an attitude, an approach to life. However, there also exists the opportunity to explore the green path through personal ritual and the creation of spells and charms.

Ritual offers you the opportunity to attune your personal energy to the energy around you in a more structured manner and to experience the natural energy of your surroundings in a different way than you do in your everyday life.

If you recognize yourself and your beliefs in the previous pages, then perhaps the path of the green witch is calling to you. If you wish to formally declare yourself to be on this path and to live the green life, you can take this oath or use it as a basis for writing your own more personal version. You may address a deity, as in this example and elsewhere in this book, or leave it out, as you prefer.

Lord and Lady,
Spirits of Nature,
Elements around me,
Bless me as I walk the path of the green witch.
May my every action be for the good of all,
For Humanity and Nature alike.
Bring me wisdom and peace,
Serenity and balance as I walk this path.
Grant me the confidence to do the work you require of me
And strength to bear the burdens life asks of me.
I swear to guard the Soul of Nature,
To work with Nature,
To honor Nature,
And all who compose nature's multitude.
These things I promise, and this I ask of you,
On this day, in this place.
As a green witch, I so swear.

If you wish, you can make this pledge anew each year at a time meaningful to you—at the beginning or end of each season, for example, to reaffirm your commitment to your path and way of life. Chapter 4 looks at the four seasons and various activities or rituals you can perform to further attune yourself to the changing energies of the yearly cycle; making this oath part of one or all four seasonal celebrations can keep your commitment fresh in your mind and spirit.

PRAYER OF THE GREEN WITCH

If the idea of a daily prayer appeals to you, this is a lovely way to begin or end your day. Try praying, aloud or in your heart, in a space that is sacred to you, one that is either formally blessed and consecrated or simply blessed by use in daily life.

Lord and Lady,
Spirits of Nature,
Elements around me,
Bless me as I move through the world today.
May I bring joy and tranquility to every life I touch.
May my actions bring only harmony to the world.
May I heal pain and soothe anger,
May I create joy and balance as I walk my path.
Support me and guide me, spirits of Nature,
This day and all days ahead of me.
This I ask of you, as a green witch,
And thank you for your many blessings.

The practice of the green witch doesn't have a lot of bells and whistles, fancy tools, or complicated rituals. Perhaps more than any other path of witchcraft, the path of the green witch rests on your philosophy of living and how you interact with the world around you. For this reason, your prayers, the rituals you perform, and your sacred space must be personally meaningful. Creating a personal practice that accurately reflects who you are and your desire to work to create harmony in the world around you is the key to living a satisfying and fulfilling life as a green witch.

Chapter 2

Embrace Your Own Power

LIKE KITCHEN WITCHCRAFT, green witchcraft emphasizes practicality and everyday activity. There are no special words, no unique prayers, no uniforms, no holy texts, no obligatory tools, and no specific holidays...unless you create them for yourself. While the green path is very much the art of daily practice, it isn't set apart as sacred. It recognizes the sacred in everyday life. The path of the green witch is sacred—very much so—but not isolated from the secular. The secular life itself is what is sacred to the green witch.

That being said, and understanding the personal nature of living the green life, the green witch path can be said to focus on certain issues and energies experienced in the secular life. Far from being simply a practice based in the use of herbs or green matter, the green witch's practice revolves around working toward establishing and maintaining harmony within herself, within her community, and with nature.

Focus on Your Energy Centers

There are seven basic areas or energies on which the green witch's practice focuses:

1. **Harmony:** within the self; between humanity and nature; between individuals; within a community or family
2. **Health:** of the body, mind, and spirit; of the immediate natural environment; of the larger environment
3. **Love:** for the self; for other individuals; for humanity
4. **Happiness:** in oneself; in others; in the natural world
5. **Peace:** within oneself; within a community or family; between factions; between nations
6. **Abundance:** personal; familial; community; nation; nature; also includes prosperity and fertility, both of which are aspects of abundance
7. **Protection:** personal; familial; community; nature

These seven areas encompass most of life. Let's look at them one by one.

HARMONY

Harmony is the watchword and main goal of the green witch's practice. Harmony can be seen as the energy that helps all the other energies flow and is capable of being applied to any of the other six areas of focus to help them along. To maintain harmony, you must balance the six other areas of your life, and when everything is in harmony, these other six areas will flow smoothly and in balance. Of course you can work toward harmony as a general goal as well, and several of the rituals, spells, and recipes in this book promote harmony.

When your personal energy is balanced and all the various parts of yourself are in tune, you are in harmony with yourself. That's harder to achieve than it sounds. We all possess traits that we dislike and wish we didn't have. It's important, however, to acknowledge those bits of your personality and spirit, for if you deny them then you are attempting to reject a part of yourself, and you thus deny part of your own energy. In doing so, you deny part of your connection to nature. Harmony between humankind and nature is important, and fostering that balance between humanity and the natural world is part of the green witch's work. Because encouraging harmony between individuals is also part of the green path, communication within humanity is one of the most common ways that energy is stirred and passed along. This communication is one of the foundations of society.

HEALTH

Health affects your physical well-being, certainly, but it also affects your emotional, mental, and spiritual well-being. Illness is a result of, or creates, an imbalance in your personal energy, which must then be rebalanced in order to return to health. Listening to and working with your own body's energy will help you maintain a balanced and healthy mind and spirit. All of these energies are interdependent and deserve to be taken into account when one or another goes out of equilibrium.

The health of your immediate environment also affects the health of your own body, mind, and spirit. Likewise, the health of the environment is a general concern for the green witch, for the environment affects all of humankind.

LOVE

Most people consider love to be an important part of their lives. They spend a lot of energy attempting to find it, keep it, or strengthen it. But there's more to love than the romantic kind that immediately pops into mind. Healthy love of the self is crucial to a well-balanced personal energy and to healthy self-esteem. Love of family and close friends who form your chosen family is also important, for it is the love of such companions that supports you in your everyday efforts. Maintaining positive and balanced relationships with these people is integral to your emotional and spiritual balance. Love for all of humanity is also an important area of focus for the green witch, even though it can be difficult to love someone you do not know personally or someone you do not like. Loving others is an example of honoring and respecting nature and all nature's creatures: it is an act of honoring their very existence and their place within nature's energy.

HAPPINESS

Like love, many people strive for happiness and joy. There are many different kinds of happiness. Your own joy, for example, is one goal, but you can also work for the happiness of others and of the natural world. While the natural world does not necessarily feel emotions as you do, there is a sense of peace and contentment to be found when an aspect of or object within the natural world is in harmony with its surroundings or with you. This state can be considered happiness. It is important to remember that happiness is very much a personal thing, and that no one act or item will make everyone happy. Happiness also encompasses the ability to rejoice and celebrate the self, and each person celebrates the self in a unique fashion.

PEACE

Peace can mean a variety of different things depending on your need: serenity, relaxation, an absence of aggression, and tranquility, for example. Like happiness, peace is a highly individual concept, and thus what constitutes peace for you may be different from how someone else defines it. When a family or community is at peace, it is balanced within itself and in harmony with surrounding communities. The green witch works for tranquility and peace, for in a peaceful environment energies that would otherwise be directed toward defense or attack of some kind can instead be directed toward more productive and positive actions.

ABUNDANCE

Abundance is an area of focus that encompasses such energies as prosperity and fertility. When you have an abundance of something, you no longer worry about it (unless it is an abundance of problems!), and you feel secure enough to focus on the areas of your life that require your attention in order to bring them into balance. If your needs are seen to, then you have the freedom to care for others. As with the other areas of focus, the green witch may look to personal, familial, and community abundance, as well as to ensuring the fertility and abundance of the natural world.

PROTECTION

Protection involves safeguarding something precious. It can be protecting your physical body or the bodies of others, your possessions, your emotional well-being, the soul or spirit of an individual, the well-being of a family or community, or the natural world, either locally or globally. When we are protected we feel safe and free to pursue other avenues of self-expression and development.

We'll return again and again to these seven categories as we explore the practice of the green witch. You will see these focal areas mentioned with recipes and rituals to help you understand the purposes for which they may be used.

Tools of Use

Because green witchcraft isn't an organized path, there are no required tools or equipment you must have in order to follow it. There are, however, important items almost every green witch uses in her practice.

HERBS AND PLANTS

With so much emphasis on working with natural energies, it is not surprising that herbs and plants immediately come to mind when one thinks about a green witch and the things she uses or interacts with. In fact, many natural objects form a part of the green witch's tool kit and supply cupboard. Chapter 5 looks at common trees, flowers, and plants used by the green witch.

YOUR HANDS

A green witch's hands are her most valuable tools. With her hands, she touches and takes in information. With her hands, she dispenses caring. Her sense of touch is a keen one. We rely heavily on sight, but our sense of touch carries great power and conveys equally important information that the green witch knows to take into account. Touch also allows us to sense energy and forms an immediate link between the green witch and that with which she communicates, whether it be absorbing information from a plant about its energy and potential uses or laying a gentle hand on the forehead of a sick child. You use your hands to tend and harvest your herbs and plants, prepare them for storage, and blend them together. Your hands can become a physical extension of your thoughts and your will.

JOURNAL

Recording your explorations, field notes, recipes, rituals, and research is of great importance because this record forms the main body of lore to which you will refer again and again in your work. Note that this journal is not a Book of Shadows, which is a term used by occultists and Wiccans to describe a record of spells and rituals and magical information. Your green witch journal will contain some magical information, yes, because the green witch understands that magic is simply another method of touching the energy of the earth; but mainly it will contain recipes, sketches, maps, experiments, observations, and accounts of your work and other experiences. Over time, you will fill many journals, and they may be messy and haphazard. That's not a problem. Your journal is not meant to be perfect. It's meant to be a real-life snapshot of your thoughts and evolving knowledge.

Recording what you learn and do means that your information will probably be organized by date. You will thus remember and understand what you did when and why; the journal provides a context for your evolution. Don't worry about the apparent mishmash of subjects you write about. As the green witch path is an organic one, it makes sense to allow your journal (like a daily diary) to meander from topic to topic. Some green witches like to separate their work into books of recipes, plant lore, and so forth so they can more easily track down information when they need to refer to it. I suggest that you put everything down in your main journal first, then copy out recipes or rituals or plant lore into another book once you've perfected them so you will have a clean and organized copy as a useful reference. It's good to have a place where you can write everything down without editing as you go: those first impressions of plants, trees, elements, and situations can be invaluable. Recopying this information later can also help you firm up your impressions and familiarize yourself with it. You will also continually be clarifying and adding new information and research.

> When you ramble in field or forest or go for walks through your neighborhood, make sure you have your green witch notebook with you. If carrying your main journal is difficult because of its size, you may wish to have a smaller field book in which to make notes while you are out. Transfer information you have picked up on your treks into your main journal when you get home again. Your green witch journal will prove important and helpful to you in months and years to come.

CUP

A simple cup (ceramic is ideal) is a useful item for the green witch. Water is one of the four physical (and metaphysical) elements, and green witches often like to have a representation of each element nearby as they work. A cup reserved exclusively to hold water in this way honors the element of water. In addition, the cup is useful to drink from in a ritual setting. While the green witchcraft practice isn't heavy on ceremony or formal ritual, a familiar tool such as a cup can lend a certain energy to your work if it is reserved only for your green witch use. Some green witches use any cup from the cupboard they feel like using at the time, because it's what's in the cup that counts.

MORTAR AND PESTLE

A mortar and pestle is invaluable for crushing dried herbs, seeds, or resins and for blending materials for a variety of projects. Although mortar and pestle sets are available in other materials, stone is the easiest to keep clean and has the weight and strength required to crush things like resins. Metal is sometimes thought to taint the energy of the herbs you crush, while wood will absorb oils and juices and be almost impossible to keep perfectly clean. Although you may like the look of a small mortar and pestle, or want to save money by buying a smaller size, do yourself a favor and don't get a tiny one. They're hard to manipulate, and if you use the mortar to blend mixtures you'll be limited to a teaspoon or two. The standard size mortar is approximately 5 inches high by about 5 inches wide, with a slightly tapered pestle of about 4 inches by 1 inch. You really shouldn't use anything smaller.

BOWLS

Also essential to your work are bowls in which to mix and hold ingredients or components while you work on various projects. An assortment of small ceramic ramekins will do for many projects, as you won't be mixing large batches of things. Make sure you have a couple of large glass bowls for larger, messier projects like mixing potpourri. Do not, however, use plastic bowls. Plastic absorbs oils and scents. Glass or glazed ceramic bowls are best.

JARS AND CANISTERS

To store your herbs, incenses, and other ingredients, glass or ceramic jars or canisters are ideal. Like your bowls, these can range in size from small spice jars to large canisters. Colored glass or an opaque material will help protect your dried herbs from fading and losing their beneficial oils. If you use clear glass, then store your jars in a cupboard to protect them from the light, or make paper cylinders to slip over them.

KNIFE OR SCISSORS

An essential green witch tool is the sharp knife used to harvest herbs and other plants. This knife must be kept extremely clean and always be sharp, for a dull blade is dangerous to both the one who uses it and that which is being cut. If you are uncomfortable using a straight knife to cut stems and leaves, you may prefer to use a pair of good sharp shears or scissors instead, reserving the knife for chopping and preparing the herbs at home on a solid and flat surface such as a table. Scissors and secateurs are easier to handle than a straight knife for some people, myself included. Again, sharpen them frequently and keep them extremely clean. Like the cup, you may use any knife that you feel drawn to using.

STAFF

A staff or walking stick not only helps you as you ramble through the natural world, but it also serves as a symbolic "world tree," which connects the material and spiritual realms. The world tree is a concept found in shamanic practice in numerous cultures around the world. The world tree is like the world's spine, serving as a support and a connection between the otherworlds and the world of humankind. In the Nordic lore, this tree, said to be an ash tree (or sometimes a yew), was called Yggdrasil. In Celtic mythology, there were several world trees, which were hazel, oak, and other woods. In shamanic practice, the world tree is often represented by a tent pole, above which are the stars of the otherworld. This tent pole is "climbed" by the shaman's consciousness through a series of meditations and other methods.

The tree is a remarkable symbol. We perceive trees as being strong and offering us shelter or support, and yet we also see them as being flexible, for some trees bend in the wind. The roots of a tree can reach deep into the earth for stability and for nourishment. Its branches reach high into the sky so that the leaves of the tree may absorb as much sunlight as possible and further nourish the tree. A staff or walking stick symbolizes all this in miniature. It is a symbol of the tree, carries a tree's energy, and reminds the green witch of the connection to both earth and sky.

Some books refer to a "stang," which is a forked staff. It is sometimes described as a sort of altar whose long single end can be thrust into the ground, leaving the forked end at the top, ready to be decorated by the green witch as desired. Garlands, sachets, bunches of herbs or flowers, and ribbons are all common things draped or tied onto stangs. The stang itself can be reused, while the decorations may be disposed of respectfully once your ceremony or action is complete.

It is interesting to compare the staff and the knife. The staff supports and serves as a connection, whereas the knife (or other blade) severs and harvests. They are two archetypal symbols, opposite and complementary. The green witch uses both and honors both the archetypes of connection and severing, unity and separation, for these are intrinsic to the cycle of life and the cycles found within nature.

COTTON OR GAUZE

A roll of natural cotton about 6 to 8 inches wide and a couple of feet long is a useful item to carry with you when you walk in forest or meadow. It may be used to roll herbs in, instead of putting them in a bag, and can help preserve more fragile cuttings. It's also good for first aid use, should you cut yourself, scratch yourself, or incur other minor damage along the way. (A small, portable first aid kit is always good to have on hand when you go out walking and exploring, and of course you should have one at home as well, either in the kitchen or the bathroom.)

POWER BAGS

As a green witch, you will over time develop a personal connection to little objects such as stones, acorns, pinecones, or fetishes, and you may wish to carry them with you. Sew up or buy a small bag to hold them, and slip it into your purse or backpack when you travel. By doing this, you carry the natural energy of those objects along with you so that they influence your own energy. You also maintain the contact with their emotional and personal meanings, which strengthen you in a different way. Together, these items form a personal power source for the practitioner. Make sure your bag isn't too big, however: if you find yourself carrying too many magical objects, it's time to sort them out and decide which are most important. Leave the items you have removed from the bag at one of your personal shrines at home in order to maintain a different sort of contact with them (see more on shrines later in this chapter).

Make Your Home a Sacred Space

In the past, the hearth served as the heart of the home. It was where heat and light were created and food was prepared. Hearth magic, or hearthcraft, revolves around safety, nurturing, and protection. Most paths have a hearth and home aspect to them, but for the green witch, so much of her spiritual practice is focused on simple home-based folk practice that hearth magic figures prominently in her green practice.

Most people on the green witch path have a strong connection to their surroundings. They instinctively seek to create an environment that supports harmony, communication, and a natural flow of energy.

Your home itself—the space in which you live—can be easily overlooked as a tool in your developing spirituality. Your home is a place of strength for you, and a place to which you should be able to return in safety to recharge your batteries. If your home is disorganized and has jarring energy, you lack that base of strength from which you must operate. One of your sources of strength and energy is already cut off from you.

TIPS FOR IMPROVING YOUR HOME

How do you make your home a sacred space? Ultimately, it depends on you and the type of energy that best supports your daily life. Here are a few tips and tricks that will make your home the best place for a green witch to live. These tips will help you keep positive energy flowing through your home.

- **Look at your décor.** How you decorate your home says a lot about you. However, you become used to how things look and sometimes forget that you never got around to painting the landlord-white walls when you moved into your apartment or that the furniture is exactly where you put it when you were just trying to get things to fit. Look at your home with fresh and critical eyes. Do the colors of the walls still reflect who you are? What does the furniture say about you? Walk through each room. Are there places you have to struggle to get to? If you don't want to go there because it's too difficult (either physically or otherwise), then chances are good that the energy flow through that area gets dammed up or otherwise slowed down. Think about rearranging the positions of furniture, pictures, and knickknacks.

- **Remove what you don't use.** If you aren't using it, throw it out. Otherwise, it's just occupying space and blocking energy. Sell it, pass it along to a friend, take it to a secondhand shop, or find another use for it somewhere else.

- **Examine your iconography.** Your paintings and photographs have a deep psychological effect on you. Take a look at the colors that dominate them, the people in them. How do they make you feel? Are they appropriate for the space they're in? As much as you love your print of Munch's *The Scream*, it may not be the best piece of art to hang in a place where you like to relax.

- **Think about the purpose of each room in your home.** When you decide what the theme or purpose of each room truly is, you can focus on removing the elements that disrupt the energy, and encourage the desired energy to remain. For example, if your living room holds your desk or home office, stores your home workout equipment, and is the repository for children's toys, you can see that there's a lot of conflicting energy there. None of it is bad; it's just confused. Try to keep each room clearly set apart for its designated purpose, and you'll find that the energy is a lot clearer. If a room serves a double purpose, keep things in their proper places.

- **Keep it clean.** Energy can seem dusty and muddy, the same way your physical home gets dirty. It's also an unfortunate fact that energy turns stale and can go bad in an environment that isn't physically clean. Housework isn't exactly the most thrilling of pastimes, but it helps keep the energy of your home bright and smooth. Make sure everything has a place, and keep it there. Keep surfaces free of dust and clutter as best you can.

- **Purify regularly.** The spiritual equivalent of physical cleaning, purification is an excellent way to maintain a good energy vibe in your home. It's also a good way to get rid of the bad feelings left over from an argument or the chaotic energy left after a party, and it removes the stray drifts of dead energy that pile up in corners or get trapped in badly laid-out rooms. You can find instructions on how to purify later in this chapter.

Sometimes we look around our homes and wonder how on earth we can make them a haven of tranquility and joy. Starting off with a good spring cleaning (even if it's fall!) is always a good idea. If addressing your whole house at once is overwhelming, do it room by room. To begin, you can choose one room to serve as a spiritual sanctuary and refuge for yourself. You can also start from the heart of your home and work outward.

Your sanctuary doesn't have to be solely devoted to you and your path; in fact, so few of us have that option that if you can pull it off, I bow to you. Most of us have to share space with members of our family and make do with carving out a little corner where we can. Even that little corner can be important for your spiritual health, however. Don't underestimate the power of a chair covered with your favorite throw next to an end table set with a candle and a small potted plant, or a window seat with pillows covered in soft or textured fabrics in colors that soothe you. If it's your space, you have a place where you can sit and close your eyes, draw that tranquility into your personal space, and find balance.

The heart of your home, on the other hand, can be easier to identify. Do people tend to end up in your kitchen when they come over? Does your family congregate in one specific room, even if another room was designed to be the family room? Where people gather is likely the true heart of your home. It's not necessarily a tranquil space and usually sees a lot of comings and goings, a lot of communication and sharing. It's the place everyone wants to be. Starting your home purification here benefits everyone who uses the space.

PHYSICAL CLEANING, SPIRITUAL PURIFICATION

The green witch has a couple of tricks up her sleeve when it comes to maintaining a healthy, happy home environment. The first is enhancing physical cleaning products with a bit of natural magic. The second is understanding that the energy in a space has to be cleaned regularly, both physically and spiritually.

The simplest way to enhance your housecleaning products is to empower them. This means filling them with extra energy associated with a particular goal. It's easy to do.

1. First hold the container of cleaning product in your hands, or hold your hands over it, and close your eyes.
2. Take three or four deep breaths to calm and balance yourself.
3. Think of the energy with which you wish to empower the product to help you attain your goal. For example, you could focus on happiness. Try to remember how you feel when you're happy.
4. Now try to pour that feeling into the cleaning product. Visualize the feeling welling up from your heart and flowing

down your arms and out through your hands; see the product absorbing that energy.

Now when you clean with it, you'll be using the physical product to clean, but while cleaning you will also be filling the area with the energy with which the product was empowered. You can empower your cleaning supplies with more than one energy as long as those energies support one another and aren't at cross-purposes. For example, you can empower a furniture polish with happiness, peace, and prosperity. For the best results, choose earth-friendly organic or fair trade cleaning products that carry no toxic ingredients.

You can do a general empowerment of your supplies, or you can think about what each one is for or what it contains, and code the empowerment that way. Chapter 5 lists correspondences associated with the scents and essences of your cleaning products. You can use these correspondences to energize your cleaning implements. For example, if your product is pine scented, empower it for protection or prosperity. If your window cleaner is scented with lemon, empower it for love and joy. If your dish detergent is scented with apple, empower it for health.

When you clean, you can further visualize the energy you are calling into the space. Visualizing while you clean also helps take away the boredom and resentment we associate with removing the dust and dirt that will just build up again anyway. Think of it as green witch maintenance of your personal space.

The second dimension to keeping your space clean and bright is purification. It's important to clean the energy of your living space because the energy of an environment affects the energy of the people functioning within it. If you've ever walked into a room and felt odd for no obvious reason, then you've been affected by the energy present in that space. While it's true that the physical state of cleanliness affects the energy of a room, you have to clean the existing energy of a room as well. Otherwise, the negative energy will pile up, just as dust collects on a bookshelf that you neglect to clean.

Purification can be done in several ways. A classic method is to sweep the negative energy away with a broom. The witch's broom is often seen only as a symbol, but it can also be used as a regular tool. It can, in fact, be a remarkably useful item, and it's very easy to use.

BROOM PURIFICATION

This basic purification with a broom can be done almost anytime and anywhere. Do not use a plastic or nylon–bristled broom. Find one with real straw bristles. Craft shops and farms open to the public sometimes sell handmade brooms. (For a personal touch, you can make one yourself following the directions in Chapter 7.) You can keep the broom you use for purification for that purpose alone, or use your regular housecleaning broom to purify. Here is how you should purify with a broom:

1. Stand in the middle of the room you intend to purify. Hold the broom in your hands.

2. Take three deep, slow breaths to calm yourself.

3. Begin to make a sweeping motion, sweeping the broom from your right to your left. Don't actually touch the floor with the broom, but swing the broom an inch or so above it. It's energy you're sweeping, not the floor itself.

4. Turning to your left, slowly turn in place. This is a counterclockwise direction, which is traditionally associated with breaking up and banishing

negative energy. Walk in a counterclockwise spiral around the room, sweeping just above the floor as you go. As you walk and sweep, visualize the energy of the room being stirred up by the motion of your broom, and any heavy spots being broken up and restored to the regular flow. See the energy being transformed from murky to bright and sparkling.

5. Sweep the entire room, gradually widening your counterclockwise spiral until you end at the door.

6. If you wish, you may end the purification with a short statement, such as: *Bright and strong flows the energy through my home. This room is purified.*

Another wonderful way to purify a room is with incense. The following recipe creates a gentle incense that, when burned, releases energy associated with clearing negativity. For more detailed information on how to make and use herbal incense, see Chapter 7.

ROOM PURIFICATION INCENSE

Burn a pinch of this incense on a small self-lighting charcoal tablet (not barbecue charcoal) in a heatproof censer or dish. This recipe will make about a tablespoon of incense.

- 1 teaspoon of frankincense resin
- 1 teaspoon of copal resin
- Mortar and pestle (optional)
- 1 teaspoon of dried powdered lemon zest
- 3 pinches of dried lavender
- Small glass jar with tight-fitting lid

1. If necessary, gently grind the resins with a mortar and pestle until the pieces are in small granules. Be careful not to overgrind them, or they will become sticky.

2. Add all the ingredients to the jar, cap it, and shake until the ingredients are well blended.

3. Hold the jar in your hands and visualize a sparkling light forming around it. This sparkling light is purifying energy to empower the incense. Visualize the sparkling light being absorbed into the blend of resins and herbs.

4. Label and date the jar. To use the incense, light a charcoal tablet and place it within the censer as instructed in Chapter 7. Take a pinch of the purification incense and sprinkle it on top of the charcoal. Place the censer in the middle of the room and allow the purifying energy to fill the room as the smoke releases it.

USING THE FOUR ELEMENTS INSIDE THE HOME

Being surrounded by nature may be the first thing that pops to mind when you think of the path of a green witch, but as you have seen, what's inside a green witch's home is just as important as what's outside. Many of us who live in an urban environment do not have access to wild areas. The modern green witch needs to figure out how to connect to green energy without being surrounded by nature. This can be easily accomplished in the home. Every green witch is different, and as the practice is informal, there is no prescribed way to decorate your personal space. Depending on your personal tastes and preferences, your home may look extremely different from the home of another green witch. One of the easiest ways to bring the energy of the natural world into your home is to introduce plants into your space.

By surrounding yourself with items of personal significance and choosing colors and décor for your home that reflect your goal of harmony and balance, you reinforce your home as your place of power. Although most green witches have one or more rooms or nooks or crannies in or around the house specifically designated as sacred locations where they work or commune with nature and the divine, your entire home can become sacred space. The hearth (the "heart" of the home) is always a focus for the home of the green witch, whether it's the kitchen or another room where the family gathers. This is rarely a convenient place for practical worship. Although green witchcraft is certainly not a ceremonial path and not laden with formal ritual, a central area through which you can touch the divine can make your spiritual journey more grounded. Shrines are ideal for this purpose.

The green witch acknowledges that the energy of the divine manifests within the natural world. The basic metaphysical building blocks of the natural world are the four elements—earth, air, fire, and water. By working with these elements, you can strengthen your connection to the natural world, and this can be done inside or outside. If you don't have access to forests and fields, you can work with the four elements indoors and balance your connection to the natural world through them.

ELEMENT SHRINES

An element shrine is a place where you can connect with one element or all four. For example, if you build a water shrine, you can include a crystal goblet of water, a small water fountain, shells, river stones, and pictures of waterfalls, rainstorms, or calm lakes. You may place a soft blue scarf under these objects and perhaps add a clear quartz crystal or two to represent ice. A fire shrine may be a collection of candles in reds and golds on a crimson cloth, perhaps with a small copper or brass figurine of a lion or a dragon. The important thing is to think about what the element means to you and to gather a small selection of items that evoke the feeling that element inspires in you. It is important to remember that a shrine is not an altar. An altar is a place of focus consecrated to the spiritual use of the green witch. It is used as a place to hold tools and equipment during a spell or ritual, and a place to work on charms and witch crafts. An altar can be permanent or temporary. Many witches set up a temporary altar each time they wish to work. As shrines may be used to honor deities or elements, the altar is not required for this purpose, and thus can be considered more of a workspace. Many green witches use whatever surface they wish as an altar, perhaps using the same cloth to spread over various surfaces each time they set up their altar. In this case, the cloth itself becomes the altar, carrying the energy associated with repeated spiritual workings.

Green witches follow their intuition, and so may not perform rituals or work spells in the same place each time, choosing the location according to what feels right for their purpose. For the green witch, this means that a workbench or a craft table may sometimes serve as an altar.

The practicality of the green witch determines where she works, and very often these sorts of tasks are undertaken in a variety of different places. Potions and salves may be created in the kitchen, while the creation of a protective wreath may take place in the garage. You may choose to formally consecrate your temporary altar each time you set it up, or not, as the mundane is sacred to the green witch. A simple blessing with the four elements can serve to consecrate the surface you have chosen to use as an altar. (See the Elemental Blessing in Chapter 7.) As a green witch, you may also consider using a stone or stump as a permanent outdoor altar in a corner of your yard or balcony, if you have one.

A shrine, however, is a place to honor something or someone or to leave offerings, a place where you can collect things of personal significance and various energies to weave together an energy that is greater than the sum of its individual parts. A shrine creates a location for a certain kind of energy. The wonderful thing about a shrine is that no one has to know what it is. It can be as simple as a photograph, a candle, a seashell, and a colored ribbon grouped together on a shelf. You know why those particular things are together; anyone else looking at them will likely think that it's simply a decorative arrangement. What's important is that the energy produced by combining these objects accomplishes the goal you envision for it.

An element shrine doesn't have to be in a place generally associated with that element. For example, you don't have to put an earth shrine outside, or a water shrine in the bathroom, or a fire shrine in your kitchen. Experiment with having four separate shrines in four different places. You can try building the earth shrine in the northern part of your house, the air shrine to the east, the fire to the south, and the water to the west, which is how they're usually associated with directions in various traditions of Western occultism. Or think about the kinds of energy you feel in various areas within your home, and site a shrine accordingly even if it's not in one of the traditional directions. If you have a room where a lot of thinking and communicating take place, try setting an air shrine there. If you have a room where everyone relaxes and feels at peace after a long day, try setting up an earth or water shrine there. Make sure to have one shrine for each element so that your home remains balanced.

If some part of your home is lacking in a certain type of energy, you can set up a shrine to an appropriate element to balance that lack. If there's a room where people tend to lose their tempers or energy runs too high, there may be an excess of fire energy that arises from its décor or as a result of how the energy flows through it. Try setting up an earth shrine or a water shrine to balance out the fire energy with stability or tranquility.

You can also experiment with creating a single shrine to all four elements. Place this shrine where it feels right to you. This may be near your own personal sanctuary, near the door so that it is the first thing you see when you enter and the last before you leave, or near the center of your home. In a shrine to all four elements, you don't need to collect multiple representations of a single element. Instead, choose one or two objects to symbolize each element and group them in an arrangement that pleases you and feels right. Shrines are fluid things; you can add objects as you feel drawn to them, or remove objects when you feel they no longer serve their purpose. On a shrine to all four elements have at least one item to represent each element at all times. Traditionally, a small dish of salt or sand holds the energy of earth, a candle holds the energies of fire, a small dish or glass of water holds water energy, and a stick of incense or feather or a fresh flower holds the energies of air. If you're worried about salt or water being knocked over, try a small potted plant or a stone for earth and a shell for water. Light the candle and the incense only when you are in the room. Doing this once a day for a few minutes can help you collect your thoughts and your energies. It gives you a moment of peace to commune with these four basic building blocks of nature.

THEMED SHRINES

By creating shrines in different places, with each shrine focused on a different energy, you can create "vortices" of specific energies that can balance out a surplus or lack of those energies in your home. Think about creating a shrine to one or more of the basic areas upon which the green witch focuses. If you wish to bring more prosperity and health into your home, for example, why not create a shrine with objects that represent abundance and health to you?

Make a Sacred Outdoor Space

If you are fortunate enough to be an urban green witch with a bit of green space behind or in front of your home, there are a few things you can do with this space to make it vibrant and more sacred.

If you own or rent land, then you may consider creating a small outdoor sacred space in which you can relax, rebalance, and reconnect with the natural world. While most people who hear the words "outdoor sacred space" envision a large circle, perhaps with standing stones and a full, flourishing garden, the green witch knows that sacred space requires nothing so elaborate. A small corner, a garden bench, or even a single stone set into a small flower bed can serve as your sacred space. You may dream of turning your entire backyard into a temple, but, in reality, your yard is more likely to be taken up by a play area for children, a toolshed, a pool, or storage. Perhaps you share your green space with others; this will also limit your activities and access. In practical terms, establishing outdoor sacred space can be an even bigger challenge than creating an indoor sacred space. If you find it a chore to keep your indoor space tidy, then an outdoor space will be no different. An entire backyard dedicated as sacred space means that you'll have to keep that entire space neat, clean, healthy, and well maintained.

Sacred space doesn't have to be obvious. It can be a small area that only you recognize as being dedicated to your spirituality. You can choose a set of plants that symbolize your practice and plant them together. You can place a stone among the plants, or a small all-weather statue, or a trellis upon which you can hang a tiny set of wind chimes. Choose anything that has meaning to you. Your small corner of outdoor sacred space should offer you a place to sit or stand to pause and clear your mind, to touch Spirit, and to rebalance yourself.

You may also find inspiration in sacred places found in nature. Areas such as streams, pools, and lakes are sometimes seen as sacred, for water is often associated with the otherworld. Perhaps a small fountain or other water feature appeals to you and can become your own sacred space. Single trees and groves have also been traditionally seen as sacred. You can plant a special tree or bush in your sacred space. Mountains are commonly held to be sacred. While building a mountain or even an earth mound is highly impractical (if not impossible), you might want to represent a mountain with one or more standing stones in any size of your choosing. Even "planting" a small 12-inch stone into the ground with intention can declare a space sacred.

The modern green witch in the urban setting can sometimes feel lost. Other options are always available. Visit your city parks or public gardens to find a place that feels comfortable and calm to you, a place where you can achieve reconnection and rebalancing. Set up a container garden on your balcony (see Chapter 6 for tips and ideas on green witch container gardening in the city). Carefully selected houseplants can also furnish you with a connection to a sacred space with the feeling of outdoors.

Be in Tune with the Earth

No matter what her access to nature is, the green witch works closely with the earth. You can live on the forty-seventh floor of a high-rise apartment building and still have a meaningful relationship with the earth.

Among the green witch's common allies are earth spirits. Earth spirits can be valuable partners and aides in your practice. An earth spirit is an intelligence or awareness attached to a particular place, a plant or tree, a natural object such as a rock or stream, or a specific type of weather. These intelligences are sometimes called devas, sometimes fairies. Often we simply refer to them as "earth spirits," "spirit of," or "force of" something. It is important to understand that these spirits are not deities.

Do all green witches recognize or work with earth spirits? No. Some green witches are comfortable talking about fairies or devas, whereas others roll their eyes and get down to hoeing the garden. Most do recognize that nature has an intelligence, or a sense of spirit, that varies according to the location. Not all of us give a name or classification to that sense of spirit.

How each green witch works with these spirits or forces depends on how she perceives them. Most green witches will agree that connecting with the various forces and energies of nature is a key aspect of their practice, but it's likely that no two green witches will be able to agree on how to do it, or even what forces they connect to. This shows how highly individualized the green practice is. One thing that most green witches would agree on is that they strive to work in harmony with these forces of nature.

How you visualize these spirits is completely up to you. You may see them as tiny people or orbs of light. You may not see them at all, but experience emotions or sensations when you are near the tree, flower, standing stone, or phenomenon with which the spirit is associated. Whether your visualization matches other visualizations is unimportant. What is important is that if you choose to work with them, you must honor the spirits as allies in your green witch work to attune to the natural world and to rebalance and harmonize life.

You can encounter nature spirits in many places and through a variety of methods. The simplest method is to reach out and connect with the spirit of a single plant, then ask the plant spirit for information on the plant's uses and properties. In his book *Plant Spirit Medicine*, Eliot Cowan stresses that the energy possessed by each individual plant is entirely personal. The information and/or gift the spirit of that plant offers to you is exactly what you need at that moment. This gift is not necessarily energy that is traditionally associated with the plant. For example, if you project your awareness to a rosebush, the energy you receive in return will not necessarily be love. The spirit of the rosebush may perceive that you require something different and offer it to you. The key to working with nature spirits like this is to be open to what they offer you without expectations or preconceived ideas. Referring to lists of correspondences associated with particular plants is useful for getting a general idea of how to use the plant's energy, but it is much more useful to communicate directly with the spirit of the plant to acquire your own understanding or interpretation of the energy and how it may be applied. The green witch never assumes she knows something, or presumes that she is correct, or takes something at face value. It is important to seek out your own experience and build your own opinions as you deepen your understanding of an element, a process, or a situation. Chapter 3 offers a series of exercises designed to help you take in information and energy through your senses, and a variety of techniques for interacting with nature and acquiring information from plant spirits.

Because there are different ways of working with plant energy, every green witch will develop her own method of absorbing and applying that energy. Employing plant energies in the practice of medicinal herbalism is perhaps the most common method of using natural energy, but the practice of homeopathy and the use of Bach flower remedies are also popular methods of working with the energy of flowers, plants, and trees.

Chapter 3

Attune Yourself to Nature

IN GREEN WITCHCRAFT, one of the most important practices is constantly reestablishing your understanding of nature as it is now around you. Maintaining contact with your physical environment is crucial to maintaining a meaningful individual practice. If you lose touch with your environment, you lose the one thing that connects you to your natural surroundings.

Green witchcraft is always about the now, about the current state of your environment. Being aware of your environment means knowing the energies moving through it, the energies it produces, its health and rate of vibration. It also means being aware of how your own energy and mental or emotional state fit into your surroundings. If you're not aware of the current state of your environment, then how can you evaluate what sort of work is required of you? You may think you know your environment, but you might be surprised when you stop to create a new relationship with it. One of the basic foundations of living the green witch path is forging a connection with nature and natural forces. It is imperative that you forge a connection with what it actually there, and not what you assume to be there.

Get to Know Your Corner of the Universe

If you live in an urban setting, then that city's energy is the energy to which you must open yourself in order to be in tune with your neighborhood and your environment. It is crucial to interact with your natural environment as it actually is, not the nature you imagine or idealize. The environment you knew yesterday or last month is no longer the environment that surrounds you: energy is in a state of constant change. Thus, the green witch must also be aware, and always adjusting her knowledge.

You may think you know your neighborhood, but it's useful to take the time to see it in a new way. Use all your senses to explore where you live. Ask yourself the following questions. Answer them honestly:

- How do the seasons change where you live? What changes can you see and feel?
- What influence does the moon have on you? What is the phase of the moon right now?
- What wild plants are common to your neighborhood? Name at least ten local plants.
- Of those ten plants, which are indigenous to your area and which were imported? When were they imported and by whom?
- What trees are most commonly found in your neighborhood? Again, which are indigenous and which were deliberately introduced? When and by whom?

- What wildlife is native to your area?
- Is the water that's channeled to your tap hard or soft?
- What type of soil does your neighborhood have? Is it chalky, clay, sandy, or other? Is it alkaline or acidic?

What you don't know may surprise you and perhaps disappoint you, too. You may know the name of the street that crosses yours, or what park is nearest to you, but what is basic and integral to your natural environment is often unknown or unrecognized. Taking the time to learn more about your neighborhood will give you a good solid base from which to learn more about how your natural environment functions.

Make a point of finding out the answers to the previous questions. Write the answers in your green witch journal.

Walking around your neighborhood with enhanced awareness can teach you more than you thought you knew. Engage in the following exercises, which are designed to help you observe as much as you can and make the most of each experience as you gather information.

INTERACTION EXERCISES

When observation is done with intent, you will discover more about your neighborhood. For this exercise, first choose a stone or a plant that you're familiar with. Allow yourself to experience it again as if for the first time. Answer the following questions. Write your answers in your green witch journal.

- What does this stone or plant feel like to the touch?
- How does it smell?
- What does it look like?
- What sounds does it make?

• How does it taste? (Caution! Try to catch the taste on the air. Never place an unidentified plant or object in your mouth.)

Once you've done this exercise with a few plants or stones you're already familiar with, try one you've not experienced before. Notes on these exercises will serve as the basis of your green witch lore and become the heart of your personal practice.

Experience the Environmental Energy Around You

Although the green witch uses herbs for their medicinal qualities, the magical qualities of the natural world are also very much her friends. If you look at the uses traditionally associated with various herbs throughout the ages, the medicinal benefits often parallel the magical uses. This is because, in addition to a certain chemical makeup that determines its effect when applied to the physical body, an herb also possesses a unique energy that affects the emotions and spirit of a person.

EXERCISE: SENSING ENERGY

Perform this exercise with a plant with which you are familiar, then try it with something you've never seen or handled before. Trust your observations. For this exercise, you'll need the plant, plus your green witch journal and a pen or pencil.

1. Take the plant in your hand. If it is a dried or harvested herb, hold a pinch in your palm or hold your hand over it, palm down. If it is a living plant that you have correctly identified as safe to touch, gently touch it with your fingers. If you cannot identify it, hold your hand above or to the side of the plant with your palm toward it.

2. Close your eyes and imagine your palm glowing. Focus on the sensation of your palm. It may tingle or grow warm or cool. That means you're focusing on the energy your palm is creating naturally.

3. Visualize the plant glowing.

4. Visualize the glow of energy collected in your palm gently stretching out to touch the glowing energy of the plant. As the two energies meet, ask yourself what you sense. Do you feel a specific emotion? Do ideas drift into your head? Thoughts or vague hunches? Pay attention. This is a method for collecting observations about the plant by sensing its energy with your own energy.

5. When you feel you have observed enough, send the plant a feeling of gratitude for its cooperation, then visualize your energy disengaging from that of the plant and drawing back into your palm.

6. Open your eyes and shake your hand firmly, as if you're shaking water off of it. This will help you get rid of any excess energy hanging on.

7. Write your observations in your green witch journal. What was the experience like? What sort of observations did you make while sensing the energy of the plant? Did the plant feel energetic, calming, nurturing? Write down everything that comes to you and don't worry about whether it makes sense or not.

Your observations of the energy of the plant are valid because they're yours. Everyone interacts differently with the energy of a plant. If lavender energizes you, then that is one of lavender's energy benefits in your practice, even though many books will tell you that lavender generally projects feelings of peace and tranquility. Acquiring firsthand knowledge is important for a green witch, as it shapes and refines your practice, personalizing it in a way that makes it truly unique.

Grounding Yourself

When you work with energy, it is important to ground. Grounding means connecting your personal energy to that of the earth and allowing a rebalancing of your energy to occur. If you are nervous or excited, you may be running too much energy through your body. The earth is a good place to shunt that extra energy. If you are lethargic or dizzy, you may be suffering from a lack of energy, and the earth has plenty to share with you. Once you are grounded, you can absorb the energy of the earth to replenish your low energy levels. To ground yourself, follow these steps:

1. Take three deep, slow breaths.
2. Next take a moment to feel your own energy flowing through your body. Focus on a point in the center of your chest and visualize a small green glowing light there. This is your energy center.
3. Now visualize a tendril of green energy growing from that energy center down toward the earth. Let it reach down past your feet. Visualize it growing into the earth itself, spreading into roots and twisting through the soil. Take a moment to feel how solid and stable your root is in the earth.
4. Now that you have formed a connection with the earth, you can either allow your excess energy to flow down to mingle with that of the earth or draw some of the earth's energy up to replace the energy you are missing.

Grounding is good to do when you get up in the morning, last thing at night, before you do any energy work, or whenever you feel a little out of sync with the world around you.

Work with the Four Natural Elements

The four physical elements form the building blocks of a green witch's understanding of the world around her. They represent the raw material of nature. The flow and interaction between the four basic elemental energies form the basis of change, transformation, growth, evolution, and development in our environment and in our lives. Each element has a specific energy. Traditionally, they have the following associations:

- **Earth:** grounding, abundance; receptive and passive
- **Air:** communication, intellect; projective and active
- **Fire:** passion, creativity; projective and active
- **Water:** emotion, sensitivity; receptive and passive

While these traditional associations are useful and a handy shortcut, how you perceive the energy of each element influences your personal practice and how you interact with the world.

EXERCISE: SENSING THE FOUR ELEMENTS

This exercise helps you build a personal relationship with each element. Before you begin, review the previous energy-sensing exercise.

- Your green witch journal and a pen or pencil
- Small dish of earth (Note: make sure it's rich earth; if all you have is dry potting soil, use a dish of salt or a stone or a crystal.)
- Hand fan (or a small piece of card stock)
- Votive candle in a candleholder
- Matches and/or a lighter
- Small dish of water
- Small towel

1. Begin by sitting quietly at a table or on the floor with the supplies set out in front of you. Take three deep breaths. As you exhale, visualize any tension leaving your body.

2. Visualize your fingertips glowing with your personal energy. Visualize the sample of earth glowing with the energy of earth.

3. Gently reach out and rest your fingertips on the soil (or salt or stone or crystal). Close your eyes and allow your personal energy to contact its energy.

4. While connected to the earth energy, observe as much as you can about how it makes you feel.

5. When you are finished, withdraw your fingers and brush them off if necessary. Shake your hand to remove any excess energy or odd sensations. Open your journal and write down all of your observations. What observations did you make about the energy of earth? How did it make you feel? What did it make you think of?

6. Pick up the hand fan or card stock in one hand, and hold your other hand out, palm up. Visualize the palm of your hand glowing with your personal energy. Close your eyes and slowly begin to wave the fan or card, creating an air current directed at your other palm. As the air moves, see it glow with the energy of air. Allow the energy of the air current to meet the energy of your palm and observe the sensations you pick up. Vary the speed of the air current and observe whether that makes a difference to your observations. When you are finished, set aside the fan and shake your hand to remove any excess energy or odd sensations. Write down your observations about the energy of the element of air in your journal.

7. Light the votive candle. Again, visualize the energy of your palm glowing. Visualize the flame of the candle glowing with the energy of fire. Hold your hand beside the flame at a safe and comfortable distance, and reach

out to the energy of fire with your own energy. Observe as much as you can about the energy of fire. When you are finished, snuff out the candle and shake any excess energy off your hand. Write down your observations about the energy of the element of fire in your journal.

8. Bring the dish of water toward you. Visualize your fingertips glowing with your personal energy, and see water glowing with the energy of the element of water. Slowly touch the surface of the water with your fingertips and allow your personal energy to engage with the water's energy. Observe as much as you can about the energy of water. When you are finished, withdraw your fingers and wipe them on the small towel, then shake them to remove any excess energy. Write down your observations about the energy of the element of water in your journal.

For a different experience, try to find a large natural manifestation of each element's energy with which to interact. Interact with the energy of the summer sun to gain a different experience of the energy of fire. Stand in a rain shower or snowstorm or next to a strong flowing river to gain a different perception of the energy of water. Bury your legs and feet in sand or take off your shoes and work your toes in freshly turned garden soil to interact with the element of earth. Stand outside on a windy day to experience the power of air. Write down your experiences and observations in your green witch journal.

To keep yourself attuned to the basic energies produced by the elements, perform this exercise at least once a year. For a deeper understanding of the cycles of energy in your area, interact with the elements on a large scale once every season. Doing this will help you better understand how the local energies interact and how their levels and presence ebb and flow with the cycle of the year.

INVOKING THE FOUR ELEMENTS

Although the four elements are always present, you can choose to recognize them in your practice by formally inviting one or more of the elements to aid you in your green witch work. This formal invitation is often called *invoking the element.*

Invoking an element is a conscious act that draws that element's energy to you in your environment. Invoking an element can be done if you want that element's particular aid or energy to blend with the work you are doing. For example, if you are creating a garden sachet for fertility in your vegetable garden, then you may invoke the element of earth to be present while you construct the sachet and weave the elemental energy into the energy of the sachet to help support and reinforce it.

> Instead of placing your elemental symbols according to one of the traditional directions, you can create a more accurate connection with your own geographic location. Where is the largest body of water in your vicinity? Where are mountain ranges? Where are plains across which the wind drives with nothing to stop it? Where does the sun seem to shine most brightly, with the most heat? You may want to reassign elemental associations with specific directions. This too can affect how you conduct personal practice.

Many green witches like to work with a symbol of each element nearby, which honors the elements and creates a balanced atmosphere in which to work. As we learned in Chapter 2, each element is traditionally associated with a cardinal direction. You can balance the overall energy of an area by introducing an elemental energy that is lacking. A small collection of all four elemental symbols supports the balance of all four energies. It also provides the green witch with a source of elemental energies from which she can draw in her magical work, if empowered to do so by those sources. Those symbols can be as simple as a small candle for fire, a feather for air (or a stick of incense to represent both fire and air together), a stone or green plant for earth, and a small glass of water. You can set them in their proper directions or in any way that appeals to you.

You can also have symbols of all four elements in your workspace where you do green witch work and formally invoke the presence of all four. If you choose to invoke all four elements, you'll have a powerful pool of energy to draw from while you work that can support your magical goal.

MEDITATING ON THE ELEMENTS

Sometimes brainstorming with other green witches (or Wiccans and other neopagans) can help you create a new set of associations for something. Relaxing and thinking about a single element at a time can also yield a surprising variety of images, thoughts, and personal correspondences. If you do this work, don't forget to have your green witch journal nearby to record ideas as they arise in your mind.

Sit comfortably in your green witch space or in another familiar and comfortable area. Choose an element and begin to free-associate. Don't do all four elements in one session, however; do them on separate days.

Discover and Develop Your Senses

While everyone interfaces differently with the world around them, we all acquire information via our five senses.

VISION

Most people are primarily visual. In social situations of every kind, we take our cues from other people. Observing their clothes, their body language, and their physical appearance we get clues how to behave appropriately. Seeing different colors also stimulates us in different ways.

Here are some exercises to help you develop how you use your sense of sight:

- **Sit in front of a window, and use it as a frame for what you see through it.** Examine everything within this frame, taking as much time as you require to really look at what you see. If you like, divide the window into quarters and examine the view, quarter by quarter. Look at textures, colors, and light and shadow. Allow yourself to really see things in detail, things you usually just glance at and take in during a split second.
- **Look at a color photo of an apple, then at a real apple.** How are they different to your eyes? How are they the same?
- **Set an everyday object on a table in front of you and look at it carefully.** Then hold it above your normal eye level and look up at it. Set it on the floor and look down at it. Move it to the left, then to the right. How does the position of the object change how you see it?

SOUND

Sound is overwhelmingly present in our lives. Traffic (cars, airplanes, etc.), the sounds of radio and television, and the noise and conversations of crowds surround us nearly all the time. Our world is very rarely truly silent. The sound of wind through the leaves of a tree or of water lapping the shoreline are sounds that speak of very specific environments that call up specific emotional reactions. Hearing helps us fill in what our vision reveals to us. If our sense of hearing is taken away from us, we feel lost, but it's also true that if we are in an area that is too quiet, we can become uncomfortable.

Here are exercises to help you deepen your sense of hearing:

- **Sit in a familiar place in your home and close your eyes.** Listen deliberately and with awareness to the sounds of your home. What do you hear? How many different sounds do you hear? Where are they coming from? Can you identify them? (Do not attempt this exercise just before you go to bed, or you will find that your attunement to little sounds will cause you to be distracted by noises all night.)

- **Sit in a public place like a mall or a restaurant and perform this exercise again.** Do it with a friend by your side so that you can relax and not worry about what's going on around you. How are the sounds different? How is the way you listen in public different from how you listen at home?

- **Sit outdoors and perform the exercise.** Do you find it more difficult to identify outdoor sounds? Where do they come from? Do you hear more or fewer sounds than you hear indoors?

TOUCH

Children are always touching everything they encounter. As we grow up, however, we learn that it isn't socially acceptable to pick up everything we see and handle it. Our concern for personal space also forces us apart. The sense of touch can be further broken down into specific kinds of senses that we often consider to come under the heading of touch: the perception of pain, the perception of temperature, the perception of pressure, the perception of balance and equilibrium, and the perception of body awareness or location.

Try these exercises to explore your sense of touch. If possible, do them with your eyes closed so you are not using sight to influence your sense of touch:

- **Gather a feather, a small bowl of salt, an ice cube in a small bowl or glass, a piece of wood, and a satin ribbon and set them on a table in front of you.** One by one, explore the touch of each item. Take as much time as possible exploring the feel of each item. Don't try to analyze the sensations: just observe and accept them, enjoying the sensory input. Pick the item up; stroke it with your fingertips, with your palm, with the back of your hand. Run it along your forearm or your cheek. Hold it in your hands and feel its weight and shape. How does it feel if you hold it still? How does it feel if you move your hand while holding it?

- **Find a patch of sun.** Move your hand into the sun and feel its warmth. Move it back into the shadows and feel the absence of heat.

- **Set a bowl of warm water and a bowl of cold water on the table in front of you.** (Make sure the warm water isn't scalding.) Sink the fingers of one hand into the bowl of warm water, leave them there for a minute, then remove them and put them into the bowl of cold water. How does the temperature contrast feel? After leaving your fingers in the cold water for a minute, dip them back into the warm water. Does the warm water feel different now?

TASTE

Our sense of taste is often drowned in excess. Fast food and canned meals have lowered our standards of taste to such an extent that if we taste a carrot freshly pulled from the earth, our taste buds are overstimulated and we lose the complexity of flavor. Even more common is biting into a fresh apple. The tangy flavor surprises our taste buds, which have become used to the duller flavor of fruit stored for periodic release over the winter and spring. Produce imported from other areas often travels for days and loses the depth of its flavor. We have become accustomed to dull, chemical-like tastes.

To remind your taste buds of single flavors, do the following exercise:

- **Wash and dry your hands.** On a table, set out a small bowl of salt, a small bowl of sugar, a small bowl of an herb such as rosemary (preferably fresh, but dry will do), a segment of orange, a slice of lemon, a glass of water, and a slice of plain bread. Sit down and touch your finger to the salt, then touch your finger to your tongue. Allow the taste of the salt to spread across your tongue. How does it taste? Can you describe it without using the word "salty"? Cleanse your palate by taking a sip of water and a tiny bite of the bread. Repeat the action with the sugar, then cleanse your palate again. Continue along through the foods, taking the time to allow each flavor to sink into your taste buds. Imagine you are tasting each food for the very first time.
- **Repeat the above exercise when you take the first bite of your next meal.** Taste each item on your plate slowly and carefully, and imagine you are tasting each one for the very first time. This is also a wonderful exercise to perform with seasonal foods such

as local fruit that has just been harvested. Strawberries grown locally and picked during strawberry season, for example, have a very special taste that cannot be replicated by hothouse berries grown across the country in the off-season.

SMELL

We usually underestimate the power of our sense of smell. Smell is a delicate sense that picks up minute shifts in air currents, and it's often overwhelmed in the city by exhaust from cars, dirt and refuse, perfumes and overscented soaps, and the general effluvia of thousands of people living close together. Alternatively, when we travel to another area, such as the seashore or the countryside, we can be overwhelmed by the odors there simply because we are not accustomed to them or because they are not diluted or covered by other scents.

Try these exercises to help deepen your understanding of your sense of smell:

- **Sit in a familiar place in your home and close your eyes.** Breathe evenly. As you inhale, notice what scents you are smelling. What is the general overall scent of your home? Can you further identify the individual smells that constitute that overall scent?
- **Repeat this exercise in a public place, with a friend along to keep an eye on what's going on around you.** When you close your eyes, how would you identify the location simply by its smell? Can you identify smaller, individual smells?
- **Repeat this exercise outdoors.** Do you find it easier or more difficult to identify individual smells outside?

THE SIXTH SENSE

Alongside the five basic physical senses, there is another method you use to gather information. This is the sense people call the sixth sense. Your sixth sense tells you that someone behind you is staring at you; even though you cannot use one of the five physical senses to confirm it, you can sense it. The green witch knows and understands that this sense cannot always be explained. She also acknowledges its existence and accepts information acquired via the sixth sense. There are various explanations for how the sixth sense works. Some say that your personal energy field (sometimes referred to as the aura) picks up the energy fields of other things and information passes between them.

Living in an urban setting, people tend to become desensitized to the sights, smells, and sounds of their daily environment. A green witch should never allow herself to become desensitized, however, because this means she will miss minute shifts in energy, changes that may signal a problem of some kind. The old adage "familiarity breeds contempt" has some application here as well. Cultivating your sixth sense can help you avoid the trap of desensitization, for it allows you an alternate method by which information comes to you.

Chapter 4

Manifest the Power of the Seasons

AWARENESS OF THE NATURAL RHYTHM of the solstices and equinoxes and how they are reflected in her own geographical location form the axis of the green witch's practice. The solar year is made up of four distinct seasons, each with resonance for the green witch. These four seasons can provide the basis for personal practice and the creation of a unique tradition specific to you as an individual green witch.

The four seasons also allow you to formally recognize the flow of seasonal energy and honor it. Set aside some time on or around the first day of the season to meditate upon the changes in energy that you are feeling in your environment. Meditate on the part of the life cycle the season represents. This chapter will provide suggested meditations for the solstices and equinoxes. They follow the traditional symbolic associations of each season.

It is important to feel the rise and fall, the ebb and flow, and the different "flavors" of seasonal energy. This is key to harmonizing the self with nature. Nature has rhythms; you have rhythms. To harmonize means to match your personal rhythms with the rhythms of your environment. This maximizes your interaction with nature so that you can communicate more clearly with it. Observe and note the rhythms of the weather where you live on a regular basis. The weather has great influence both over your environment and over your own personal energy.

Seasonal Cycles and Energy

No matter where you live, your weather cycles form a recognizable pattern over a full calendar year. The vegetation grows and falls back in a pattern over the year. The animal population follows certain behavioral patterns. As the earth's angle and distance from the sun change, the seasonal cycle embodies the basic relationship between light and dark. The concept of darkness is necessary in the natural cycle: without darkness, there can be no fallow period during which the earth regains its strength, seeds will not germinate, animals will not bear their young in season.

When we observe the four seasons, we can categorize the climate shifts and environmental responses that occur over the calendar year. When we observe a certain event happening in the natural world, for example, we can say, "Ah, now it is spring." That event may be different for your neighbor, for someone in the next time zone, or someone in the other hemisphere or south of the equator. We all have personal associations with seasonal events that really bring home what time of year it is. These associations are part of our personal connection with the natural world around us.

In North America and Europe, there are four seasons that begin on specific days and at specific times. Climate changes are created by the orbit of the earth around the sun. As earth orbits the sun, the earth's surface is exposed to more or fewer of the sun's effects. This is caused by the angle of declination of the axis of the planet. The amount of sunlight triggers behavioral responses in plants and animals, including humans.

In ancient cultures, the seasons were often named according to the natural phenomena of the geographic location and were often calculated through observation of the movements of stars and planets, or events such as flooding or the movements of herds. Today, in some areas the seasons are classified by temperature (the hot season, the cold season) or by meteorological events (the rainy season, the dry season).

In North America, although the seasons are determined by the astronomical position of the sun and the earth, meteorologically the approximate dates March 21, June 21, September 21, and December 21 are used to mark the beginning of spring, summer, fall, and winter. If a different date in these months makes more sense to you where you live and corresponds to how seasonal differences manifest in your environment, why not use them? The point of living as a green witch is to be in tune with your surroundings. Adhering to a date simply because it is a standard date does not always make sense when it comes to celebrating the changing seasons. If spring arrives earlier or later than March 21 in your area, as reflected in the plant and animal kingdoms and in your own soul, then by all means, celebrate the beginning of spring at a different time. Spring doesn't have to come on the same day every year, either. Perhaps one year you sense that spring has arrived on April 2, for example, and the next year you feel that it has already arrived on March 12. Trust your instinct. It is responding to the energies flowing through your locale.

As the green witch lives a practical life, the four seasons offer both practical and spiritual opportunities for learning more about nature and living in harmony with it. The beginnings of the four seasons are specific points at which to pause and evaluate your life. This isn't only useful for spiritual evaluation; it's also good for practical purposes, such as cutting back the dead growth in the garden, pruning trees, harvesting the last of your crops, washing windows, clearing out the garage, and doing general housecleaning.

The true feelings of the season can arrive earlier or later than the calendar indicates. It is up to you as a green witch to observe, trust, and choose to celebrate when you feel the season has truly arrived. Remember, the key to developing your own personal practice is forging your own connection with the energy flow of the year as it is influenced by the weather and climate where you live. If you live south of the equator, remember that these equinoxes and solstices are reversed, and use the appropriate meditation for your season.

TIDES OF THE YEAR

The seasonal tides echo the natural cycle in the inner life of the green witch.

1. Spring equinox to summer solstice: the growing tide
2. Summer solstice to autumn equinox: the reaping tide
3. Autumn equinox to winter solstice: the resting tide
4. Winter solstice to spring equinox: the cleansing tide

These four tides may be seen as stages of your life. The cyclic nature of life is reflected in your relationships and careers and what you learn as you grow. You can imagine it as a spiral. The energies of seasonal tides give the green witch opportunities to look inside herself and see all nature reflected in miniature there.

Celebrating the Solstices and Equinoxes

In your personal practice, it is better to observe how you feel for a year and base your own festivals on those observations than it is to consult a book, find out that it is the fall equinox, read that it is associated with endings and harvests, and celebrate accordingly. What if you think of fall as a beginning? While celebrating the age-old associations can be positive, in that it nurtures a sense of unity with your ancestors and with the earth, it can also be counterintuitive if it does not coincide with the energies of your geographic locale. A green witch seeks to honor the energies to which she is seeking to attune herself.

Green witchcraft is about being hands-on, about nurturing and developing our relationship with the natural world around us. The green witch makes her own tools, and grows and harvests her own herbs. By directly interacting with the natural sequence of seasons, you create a larger practice. By understanding how the year ebbs and flows, you gain a deeper understanding of how life itself weaves, unravels, and reweaves the web of life.

So how do you celebrate a solstice or an equinox? There is no right or wrong way. There are no formal traditions that must be marked, no rituals that must be enacted. Every green witch creates her own tradition, her own expression of the seasons and how they change. That unique expression will reflect how the season affects her spirit, her heart, and her body.

The most basic way to celebrate the solstices and equinoxes involves allowing yourself to interact with the natural environment around you. Spend the day outdoors. Go for a walk through your neighborhood and look at how things are changing. If you prefer, you can celebrate indoors. Gather seasonal greenery and decorate your home. While some green witches believe that nature's bounty should be left outdoors and appreciated in its place and not be harvested for something as minor as decorating, others advocate using flowers and greenery as they are available and always with a sense of harmony, responsibility, and fair use.

Meditations for Every Season

Meditating at each seasonal shift is one of the most direct ways of experiencing the energy of the natural world and tracing your own response to its ebb and flow throughout the year. Use the following seasonal meditation outline as the basis for your meditations. Appropriate seasonal variations (as listed in the section on each season) are given. Using a consistent meditation with only these small variations lets you easily sense the minor differences that come out of the meditation that you might otherwise miss if you followed a different sequence each time.

SEASONAL MEDITATION BASE

Ideally, this meditation should be done outside: in your garden, in a private and secure spot in a public park, even on your balcony or your patio. If you have access to forests or fields, these too make ideal places in which to encounter and attune to the energy of spring. If you choose to meditate in a public place, make sure that you are comfortable and feel safe enough to allow yourself the freedom to meditate. If you are concerned about others interfering, go somewhere else or do the meditation in your home.

1. Settle yourself comfortably and close your eyes. Visualize a fine green mist rising from the ground and radiating out from all the growing things around you.

2. Take three slow, deep breaths. Each time you inhale, visualize that mist of verdant green energy flowing into your lungs and spreading through your body, bringing with it the feeling of comfort and relaxation, of oneness with your surroundings. As you exhale, release any tension, stress, or worry you may be feeling.

3. Allow your personal energy to expand slightly so that it merges with the natural green energy around you. Direct your awareness downward into the soil. Allow it to sink deep into the earth, slowly and gently. Do not force your energy, but let it sink and sift through the particles of earth. When you feel comfortable, stop and feel the energy of the soil around you cradling you, enfolding you.

4. *Insert the appropriate seasonal visualization here.*

5. When you feel it is time to return to normal consciousness, offer the soil around your awareness a small gift of gratitude (emotion is energy, after all), then allow your awareness to slowly rise up through the soil to return to your physical body. After spending time within the earth like this, you will probably be so relaxed that slow movement will be natural to you. Make sure that you take the time to return thoroughly. Do not simply snap yourself back, or you will be disoriented and your personal energy will be unbalanced.

6. Once your awareness has returned, ground yourself (see Chapter 3) and take three deep breaths.

7. Open your eyes and gently move your arms and legs to warm them up and to reaffirm your physical form. Stand up slowly and do a few gentle stretches to loosen up your muscles.

Write a summary of your experience in your green witch journal. How did it feel to interact with the earth at this season? Did the interaction teach you anything new? Did you learn anything new about your geographic location? Did you pick up any insight from the experience? Write down your thoughts and questions, any visions you may have had or new understandings you may have come to. Make notes on how you feel as this season begins, what the energy of the location you chose felt like. Remember to note the weather, too.

In future years, you can make reading notes in your witch's journal the beginning of your seasonal celebration. Compare how you feel now to how you felt in previous years. What are the similarities? What are the differences?

THE VERNAL EQUINOX

The movement of the seasons is a never-ending cycle. Although in reality there is no place that we can firmly point to as the beginning of the seasonal cycle, spring is often seen as the first season in the sequence. This comes from the fact that earlier calendars began the year in the spring. Spring is also traditionally associated with new beginnings, sowing, childhood, and young things in general. Spring is a time of potential, a time for planning and planting, and a time for making wishes about what you want the future to hold. The vernal equinox can be likened to the dawn of the day. New light emerges, touching the landscape with a gentle glow, and life brims with wonderful possibilities simply waiting to be realized.

The vernal equinox takes place at the moment when night and day are of equal length for the first time after the winter solstice. From this moment on, the sun will be in the sky for a few more minutes every day, and nights will slowly become shorter.

SPRING MEDITATION

Perform this meditation on or around the spring equinox. If the day of the official equinox doesn't work for you, try it around the time of year when there are many new things emerging in the natural environment where you live.

Begin the meditation as outlined in the seasonal meditation structure.

Once you have reached a place of comfort deep inside the earth, breathe in that energy and feel it fill your body. Feel the soil's energy at this time of the spring equinox. Feel the potential that vibrates in the earth. Reach out and sense the first movements of roots and seeds where they curl in safety, absorbing the soil's energy and using it to nourish their own life force, growing stronger in their sleep. Sense the slow awakening of these roots and seeds, and think about the potential they hold and the luxurious life they will soon display.

Remain cradled by the energy of the soil as long as you like, enjoying the feeling of potential and the first stirrings of life.

Finish the meditation as outlined in the seasonal meditation structure.

THE SUMMER SOLSTICE

The summer solstice, or midsummer, marks the moment when the sun is at its highest. It is the day when the sun spends the most hours above the horizon. Traditionally, this day is associated with expansion and great energy. The summer solstice marks the beginning of summer, a period in today's busy world that we nostalgically associate with play and relaxation and summer vacations. Conversely, it is also associated with hard work, for in the agricultural cycle the fields must be tended. Crops continue to mature quickly and with great strength and can easily grow out of hand.

SUMMER MEDITATION

Perform this meditation on or around the summer solstice, or whenever you sense summer has arrived where you live. If this doesn't work for you, try it around another time of year when things are in the middle of a period of growth and expansion.

Begin the meditation as outlined in the previous seasonal meditation structure.

Once you have reached a place of comfort deep inside the earth, breathe that energy in and feel it fill your body.

Feel the soil's energy at this time of the summer solstice. Feel the energy of nourishment and growth that vibrates in the earth. Sense the expansion, the throb of life as it flows through roots and stems. Explore the interactive system of minerals, nutrients, water, and fertile decomposed vegetable matter that feeds the new generation of plant life. Sense the feeling of vitality, of life, of expansion and increase, of reaching up and opening out, the flow of passionate and joyful creation that pulses through the land.

Remain cradled by the energy of the soil as long as you like, enjoying the feeling of vitality and fertile life around you.

Finish the meditation as outlined in the seasonal meditation structure.

THE AUTUMNAL EQUINOX

As at the vernal equinox, the minutes of day and night are precisely equal at the moment of autumnal equinox. From the summer solstice, the minutes of daylight have slowly decreased and the minutes of night have increased.

Fall is traditionally associated with harvest and thanksgiving for the bounty of the earth, which has been tended from even before plants began to grow. Fall also incorporates themes of sacrifice, loss, and gentle regret, for the precious days of summer have passed and winter now approaches. Autumn is a time of weighing. What is necessary to keep? What can be left behind as the cycle passes to a time of scarcity?

FALL MEDITATION

Perform this meditation on or around the autumnal equinox or whenever you sense that fall has arrived where you live. If this doesn't work for you, try it around the time of year when things are in the middle of a period of fulfillment and harvest and nearing the end of their cycle.

Begin the meditation as outlined in the seasonal meditation structure.

Once you have reached a place of comfort deep inside the earth, breathe that energy in, and feel it fill your body.

Feel the soil's energy at this time of the autumnal equinox. Feel the energy of completion and contentment that vibrates in the earth. Reach out and sense the fullness, the feeling of achievement as it flows through roots and stems. Explore the gentle, slower movement of energy throughout the soil and the roots of plants as the cycle of producing fruit and seed comes to an end on the surface of the earth.

Sense the feelings of contentment, of life, of pleasure and satisfaction, of appreciation and offering that pulse through the land.

Remain cradled by the energy of the soil as long as you like, enjoying the feeling of plenty and serenity around you.

Finish the meditation as outlined in the seasonal meditation structure.

THE WINTER SOLSTICE

The winter solstice is the shortest day of the year, when the sun's height is the lowest that it is all year. Although the hours of night outnumber the hours of daylight, from this moment on, the sun begins to regain its lost time.

Winter in the life cycle is traditionally associated with apparent death, which is necessary to enable the rebirth associated with spring. Without death, there can be no new life.

WINTER MEDITATION

Perform this meditation on or around the winter solstice, or whenever you sense that winter has arrived where you live. If this doesn't work for you, try it around the time of year when things have reached a point of rest, of apparent death or cessation of motion.

Begin the meditation as outlined in the previous seasonal meditation structure.

Once you have reached a place of comfort deep inside the earth, breathe that energy in and feel it fill your body.

Feel the soil's energy at this time of the winter solstice. Feel the energy of quiet and stillness that permeates the earth. Reach out and sense the darkness, the feeling of slowness as it flows through roots and stems. Explore the barely perceptible movement of energy throughout the soil and roots as the world above lies sleeping. Sense the feelings of relaxation, of incubation, of dreams and the breath of what may become that trickle through the land.

Remain cradled by the energy of the soil as long as you like, enjoying the feeling of warm stillness and sleep around you.

Finish the meditation as outlined in the seasonal meditation structure.

Performing Seasonal Rituals

Meditations are one method of interacting with the energy of the season. Rituals are another. Because green witchcraft is informal, whether to use the popular neopagan practice of creating a ritual circle to set the ritual site apart from the mundane world is up to the green witch herself. In occult traditions, the circle represents protection from negative forces that could interfere in your work. In the green witch's practice, however, we do not require protection, for everything is part of nature. Instead, those who choose to use a circle use it to designate an area of purity in which to work, a sacred place set apart for the ritual. If you choose to delineate your ritual area in this fashion, you may simply walk the perimeter of your space with the intent of marking it. No further formal action, visualization, or words are required.

Spring Equinox Egg Ritual for Welcoming Creative Energy Into Your Life

This ritual is designed to gather up some of the abundant, fertile energy of nature in the springtime and direct it toward an area of your life where you could use a shot of productive, creative energy.

This spell appeals to the spring maiden and the youthful sun for their blessings and energy; I have deliberately used symbolic figures in this ritual so that you can visualize them as you desire. Because green witchcraft does not worship any specific deities, you are free to invoke deity energy as you see fit and according to your religion of choice. In this and other rituals, if you wish to appeal to a deity whom you worship on a regular basis, then by all means substitute that god or goddess.

Before beginning this spell, color your uncooked egg according to your personal color associations. For example, if the area of your life which requires energy is career related, you might color the egg brown or orange; if it is related to romance, you may wish to color the egg red or pink.

Perform this ritual in your home at your altar, or wherever you feel comfortable. You will need:

- Matches or lighter
- 1 small, pale green candle
- 1 uncooked egg, colored according to your preference
- Pen
- Small piece of parchment
- Heatproof dish

Then follow these steps:

1. Create sacred space however you prefer to do so.

2. Light the candle and take the egg into your hands. Say: *Maiden Goddess of Spring, light, and life, Youthful God of the Sun, exuberant and joyful: Bless this egg, and fill it with the power of spring, of life, of fertile and creative energy. May my life be energized!*

3. Set the egg next to the candle.

4. Using the pen, write on the parchment the situation or area of your life to which you wish to direct the creative energy of spring. When you have finished writing, hold the paper between your hands and empower it with your need.

5. Carefully touch the corner of the paper to the candle flame until it catches fire. Drop it in the heatproof dish and allow the paper to burn completely to ash.

6. Allow the candle to burn down completely. Let the egg rest beside the candle.

7. When the candle has gone out, take the egg and the bowl of ashes outdoors and dig a hole in the ground. Place the egg in the hole and sprinkle the ashes of the paper on top of it. Bury these carefully and with reverence. The energy of the egg and the earth will slowly begin to infuse the situation in your life that you asked to be energized.

SUMMER GARDEN BLESSING RITUAL

Making flower chains is a wonderful way to combine play, work, and creativity. Take advantage of the abundant and luxurious energy of expansion and growth that manifests in the summertime to bless your garden with this ritual. Before you begin, select a place in your garden to serve as a place of offering. Gather the leaves and flowers you will be using from your garden or the wild (remembering to harvest responsibly); do not buy them from a florist. If you wish, use your hand instead of the staff or wand. You will need:

- Wand or staff
- Stang (forked staff or stick; see Chapter 2)
- 12 flowers (your choice; wildflowers and weeds are fine, but make sure the stems are at least 4 inches long and do not select anything with toxic leaves)
- 12 leaves (your choice; as large as possible, with firm stems)
- Knife or scissors (optional)
- Pitcher, bowl, cup, or watering can full of water

Then follow these steps:

1. With the wand or staff in your hand, circle around or walk through your garden. Hold the wand or staff in front of you, its base close to the ground. Visualize the life energy as it rises up from the soil through the plants' roots to nourish the stems, leaves, flowers, and fruit.
2. Circle or walk through the garden a second time, still holding the wand or staff, but this time raised higher so that the tip reaches into the sky. Visualize the energy of the sun and the rain nourishing the plants from above.
3. Circle or walk through the garden a third and final time, now holding the wand or staff horizontally. Visualize the energy of each individual growing plant expanding to join with the other plants around it, forming the whole of your garden.

4. Lay down the wand or staff in front of your chosen place of offering. Take up the stang, and insert the single end into the earth firmly so that the forked end stands upright and stable.

5. Sit or kneel in front of the stang and take up one of the flowers. Strip away any leaves or greenery along the stem and trim it to approximately 6 inches long. With your fingernail (or the knife or scissors, if you prefer), make a small vertical slit in the stem about 1–2 inches below the petals. Don't make the slit too long; ½ inch ought to be enough. Do the same to the other eleven flowers.

6. Hold the first flower just below the petals. Pick up a second flower and carefully insert the end of the stem into the slit in the first flower. Carefully pull the stem of the second flower through the slit until the slit in the second stem has passed through the first stem's slit.

7. Pick up a third flower and insert its stem into the slit on the second flower. Repeat until all twelve flowers have been assembled into a chain.

8. Gently hang the flower chain on the stang by laying each end over one of the branches so that the middle of the chain forms a gentle swag. If the chain is not long enough, simply hang it over the fork itself.

9. In each of the leaves, make a tiny slit in the stem of the leaf.

10. Take one leaf and hold it in your hand. Take a second and gently insert the stem into the slit of the first leaf. Pull the second stem through until the slit passes through the first slit. Continue with the remaining leaves, until you have another chain.

11. Gently hang the leaf chain on the stang by laying each end over one of the branches, so that it lies along the flower chain. If the leaf chain is not long enough, simply hang it over the fork or gently twine it around the flower chain.

12. Lay both your hands on the chains and say:

    Powers of Wind and Earth,

    Powers of Sun and Rain:

    By tree and flower and leaf,

    With my hands and heart,

    I bless this garden with life and love.

13. Take up the pitcher or bowl of water and walk through your garden, gently sprinkling drops of the water throughout. Keep some water back. Return to the stang and pour the last of the water at its base where it has been thrust into the ground and say: *I give thanks to the earth for its bounty, its protection, and its support. Blessed be the earth and those who walk upon it.*

14. If you like, you can sit by the stang and meditate for a while or simply enjoy being in your garden. You can also weed, work the soil, thin out some plants, or do whatever gardening needs to be done. Leave the chains on the stang for at least a day (or as long as you feel right in leaving them). Remove them when they have wilted, but do not throw them out. Add them to your compost pile.

AUTUMN EQUINOX HARVEST RITUAL

This ritual honors the earth's produce and bounty and allows you to participate in the season's energy by performing the essential harvesting action. You can harvest something from your own garden or something wild. If you have a lot to harvest, choose the first or the last item you plan to harvest for this ritual. The harvesting tool will depend on what you are harvesting. You will need:

• Sharp knife, secateurs, scissors, or shears
• Small bottle or bowl of water

Then follow these steps:

1. Standing next to what you are harvesting, reach out with your hand and sense that plant's energy. Say:

    I honor you, earth's child.

    I honor your growth, your flower, and now your fruit.

    I thank you for your energy.

    Blessed be, earth's child.

    May I who harvest your fruit be blessed by the act.

2. With the harvesting tool, cut the fruit off the plant. Sense the energy of the plant when you have harvested its produce. Honor the difference you feel.

3. Pour the water at the base of the plant in thanks.

ICE RITUAL FOR THE WINTER SOLSTICE

This ritual is a physical reminder that spring will always follow winter. If you live in a region with no snow, make a batch of ice cubes prior to the ritual and use those. A metal bowl is recommended because it will best reflect the candle's flame, although it will grow very cold, so be aware of your fingers when you hold it. If it's wintry cold where you live, perform this ritual indoors. Otherwise, the ice and snow will not melt, and the point of the ritual will be lost.

Perform this ritual in your home at your altar or wherever you feel comfortable. You will need:

- Bowl (preferably metal)
- Ice cubes or chunks of ice and snow from outdoors (approximately 1 cup)
- Candle (red, orange, or yellow) in candleholder
- Matches or lighter

Then follow these steps:

1. Place the snow or ice cubes in the bowl and sit or kneel next to it. Light the candle and place it behind the bowl so that you can see the flame's reflection dancing in the ice or snow.
2. Say:

   As the season turns, and the sun shines,
   I hail the light that returns to the land.
   Darkness ebbs, light again flows,
   And day by day the land will grow warm.
   Welcome again, bright sun!
   May your beams caress the land and transform ice to water,
   Snow to rain, cold to warmth,
   And winter to spring again.

3. Allow the snow or ice to melt until it is water. Look at the reflection of the candle flame on the water in the bowl and think about the warmth of the sun. Feel the energy of the snow as it melts, the energy of the flame as it emits light and heat. Observe the communication between the two.
4. When you are finished, pour the water outside at the base of a tree.

Part 2
Walking the Green Path

Chapter 5

Live Closely with the Earth

THE SOURCES OF THE GREEN WITCH'S information, wisdom, and power are the different aspects of nature and the natural system—the luminaries in the sky above, the plant world, the mineral world. Using the bounty of nature in a personal spiritual practice offers the reward of knowledge and insight acquired through experience. This chapter looks at how the green witch uses the various elements of nature, including the sun and moon, trees, stones, flowers, and herbs.

A green witch interacts with nature itself to receive the full benefit of its teachings. Reading about nature, watching television documentaries, and listening to lectures may all be excellent ways to acquire knowledge, but firsthand experience of nature is always the best teacher. However, nothing comes free. There is always an exchange of energy. What do you exchange for this wisdom that you glean from nature? Your dedication to your work. Your willingness to work to heal the earth and its creatures, including humankind, and to restore harmony between them. Your willingness to pass your knowledge on to others.

The Sun, the Moon, and the Stars

The sun, the moon, and the stars have long been looked to for power and aid. Wicca, one of the most prevalent forms of modern nature worship, places great emphasis on working with the phases and energy of the moon. The green witch knows that while seeds may be sown according to lunar phases and that they sprout and are nurtured in the dark, they also grow and thrive thanks to the warmth and energy of the sun.

The sun enables life to thrive on this planet. It provides heat and light and nourishes you on a very basic level. You depend on the sun for your life. Very often, however, we take the sun for granted or note its existence only in connection with the weather. However, the green witch who lives in an urban setting can always connect with the sun, even if there isn't a scrap of green space around.

In the Western occult tradition, the sun is usually associated with power, success, prosperity, health, joy, family, creativity, growth, and expansion. Solar energy changes throughout the day. The energy of the early morning sun, for example, is not the same as the energy of high noon, nor of late afternoon. Dawn and sunset have completely different energies. Generally, the four key solar points (dawn, noon, sunset, and midnight) correspond to the stages of life as seen in the four seasons: birth, maturity, old age, and death. Do not, however, let this stop you from working with the sun all day long. There are other factors that you can take into account, and your own instinct is more immediately pertinent to your own work than traditional associations. If you feel drawn to using solar energy at sunset to launch a new project, then by all means do it!

Solar energy can also be affected by where the sun is in the earth's orbit. As the earth moves, twelve different constellations of stars pass above you, and the sun appears to move through them. Depending on which constellation is highest at a given time, the sun is said to be "in" that constellation. For example, the sun moves into the constellation of Cancer, the Crab, on the summer solstice. These constellations, of course, make up our astrological zodiac, which is a method of divination that uses the position of stars and luminaries to determine hidden information and influences. When the sun is "in" each constellation, that constellation's associated energy is said to add a slightly different spin to the basic solar energy.

ZODIAC ENERGY CORRESPONDENCES

- **Aries, the Ram:** action, new beginnings
- **Taurus, the Bull:** manifestation, material things, physical comfort
- **Gemini, the Twins:** communication, intellectual work
- **Cancer, the Crab:** family, nurturing, the home
- **Leo, the Lion:** success, luxury, leadership
- **Virgo, the Virgin:** practicality, organization
- **Libra, the Scales:** society, people
- **Scorpio, the Scorpion:** passion, justice
- **Sagittarius, the Centaur Archer:** study, exploration
- **Capricorn, the Goat:** business, foundation
- **Aquarius, the Water-Bearer:** invention, innovation
- **Pisces, the Fish:** spirituality, mysticism

At different times of the year, stellar influences add a dash of flavor to solar energy. Each period of the zodiac lasts approximately thirty days, and the sun transits into the next constellation on or around the twenty-first of each month. Appropriately enough, in astrology, these are called sun signs. (The moon also appears to pass through these constellations, spending approximately a day and a half in each, and lunar energy is similarly affected by the stellar energy. In this instance, they are called moon signs.)

MEETING THE SUN

The most basic way to experience the sun's energy is to go outside and stand or sit in the sun. Be careful, however. Do not look directly into the sun and be sure to protect yourself from sunburn by wearing protective clothing and/or sunscreen of an adequately high SPF.

- To receive solar energy, settle yourself comfortably in a sunny spot and close your eyes.
- Visualize a fine green mist rising from the ground and from all the growing things around you.
- Take three slow, deep breaths. Each time you inhale, visualize that mist of verdant green energy flowing into your lungs and spreading through your body, bringing with it the feeling of comfort and relaxation, of oneness with your surroundings. As you exhale, release any tension, stress, or worry you may be feeling.
- Open your awareness to the warmth of the sunlight. Just receive it, let it in. Absorb whatever energy it offers to you. How does it feel physically? Emotionally? Spiritually? Does the sunlight have a message for you?
- Take as long as you wish to commune with the sun and its energy. When you are finished, take a final three deep breaths and open your eyes. Be sure to stretch and shake out your arms and legs before standing up or moving suddenly.

In your green witch journal, write a summary of your experience. How did it feel to touch the energy of the sun? Did you pick up any insight from the experience? Write down your thoughts and questions, any visions you may have had, and any sudden understandings you may have come to.

To achieve further insight into the sun's energy and how it changes, here are exercises for exploring and attuning to solar energy:

- For one day, pause for at least five minutes at dawn, noon, sunset, and midnight to observe the movement and feeling of the energy where you live. Write your observations and experiences in your green witch journal and compare the different energies of the key solar points of the day.

- For one day, meditate at each key solar time. Open yourself to the sun's energy and sense it as directly as possible. Be aware of what happens. Make notes in your journal after each meditation. Wait a day, then compare how you felt or the information you received after each meditation.

- For one day, perform the same basic ritual at each key solar time. Write down your experiences and feelings after each ritual. Wait a day and compare similarities and differences in the four rituals.

- For a deeper exploration, do the same exercises once during each season. How does the sun's energy change over the cycle of a day? During the year?

THE MOON

The moon is usually associated with the hidden, more mysterious practices of witchcraft. Lunar mysteries have their place in the life of the green witch, who knows that ordinary life itself is a sacred mystery. Traditionally, the moon's energy is associated with feminine power, dreams, psychic ability, mystery and hidden knowledge, travel, children, spirituality, mysticism, the seas and oceans, and transformation.

The phases of the moon are important in agricultural practice. Sowing and harvesting were once done according to the phases of the moon, and (depending on the individual) sometimes still are. Scientifically, this may have something to do with the moon's proven influence on water and other fluids. Plants are composed of a large amount of water, which implies that their life cycle would be affected by the moon's phases.

These basic rules may be applied to gardening during the phases of the moon. In general, plant things whose strength lies above ground while the moon is waxing and those whose strength lies below ground while the moon is waning.

- **New to first quarter:** plant leafy annuals and herbs
- **First quarter to full:** plant flowering annuals, above-ground vegetables and fruit, and vines
- **Full to third quarter:** plant perennials, root vegetables, and bulbs
- **Third quarter to dark:** weed, maintain, cultivate, and fight pests and disease

If you pay attention to the phases of the moon, you can also determine good times to perform both spiritual and secular actions in your garden. The following phases correspond to phases in the life cycle of a plant:

- **New moon:** seeds
- **Crescent moon:** shoots and sprouts
- **Waxing moon:** growth and flowering
- **Full moon:** fruit
- **Waning moon:** harvest
- **Dark moon:** cutting down a dead plant to prepare for new growth

The moon appears to move through the constellations just as the sun does, and moon signs are also said to have an effect on the work you do in your garden. Some signs are more favorable for certain kinds of work than others. The moon appears to pass through all twelve constellations in approximately twenty-eight days and spends a day and a half to three days in each sign:

- **Plant:** moon in Cancer, Scorpio, and Pisces
- **Harvest:** moon in Aries, Gemini, and Leo
- **Cultivate:** moon in Virgo, Sagittarius, and Capricorn

Any green witch interested in how the plant world responds to the lunar cycle should keep a farmer's almanac handy.

MEETING THE MOON

To explore the moon's energy, do the exercises for meeting the sun, but at night. Make notes of your experiences. Try these variations on the exercise to further explore lunar energy and deepen your attunement.

Perform this exercise at the same hour of the night, four times during one lunar cycle: during the waxing phase, at the full moon, during the waning phase, and at the dark moon. Make notes of your feelings and experiences in your journal. How does the lunar energy change during the cycle?

Perform this exercise on the full moon for all thirteen moons in the calendar year. How does the lunar energy change as the seasons shift?

Working with Green Energy

A large part of the green witch's path consists of using the natural energies contained within plants and trees to attain a certain goal, be it medicinal or magical. Those who follow a path linked to natural magic have long known that we can weave these energies into our everyday life to harmonize ourselves or others with the energy flow of the world around us.

Training yourself to work with these energies takes more than memorizing a list of correspondences. As always, hands-on experience is the best way to learn how you work most effectively. Interacting with a plant while it is still growing and interacting with its energies after it has been harvested will give you a good idea of what this plant can be used for and to what applications its energy is best suited. Books on herbs, flowering plants, indoor and outdoor plants, and trees can be useful as references and general guides, but, ultimately, your energy readings and your instinct will determine how you can best use the energies of the natural world. (Please note that I am referring to the magical application of these items, not medicinal applications. To become competent in herbal medicine, you must take accredited courses in medicinal herbalism, and/ or work responsibly with a reliable book.)

The first thing you need is at least one good handbook on the native flora where you live. This isn't a book on the magical or medicinal applications, but simply a guidebook to identifying the plants and trees.

Before you begin to work with plants, you should know the basic rules of wildcrafting. Wildcrafting is the harvesting of plant matter from the wild, as opposed to harvesting cultivated plants. Why wildcraft? Because there are some plants you can't grow in a garden. They defy the cultivator's hand. In addition, few green witches are able today to plant every single herb, tree, flower, or shrub they wish to use in their practice. The basic rules for ethical wildcrafting are as follows:

- **Never harvest all of anything.** In fact, don't even harvest half of it. A good rule is to harvest only a quarter of what you see, as long as there is plenty of it and it is growing abundantly, and then only if you absolutely need it. It's better to go back for more fresh material than to be stuck with a huge pile of dried herb you harvested "just in case." You will probably throw it out. Don't waste it.

- **Remember that harvesting wild plant matter can very easily lead to trespassing on someone else's land.** Look for signs. When in doubt, ask.

- **Picking protected plants is illegal.** Make a point of familiarizing yourself with the local laws on harvesting wild flora. Find out what the protected species of your area are and help protect them.

- **Think clearly at all times.** If you travel to harvest wild plants, research the specific region you are traveling to. Know the roads and paths, the dangers and the safe areas. Make an itinerary and stick to it. If you're going into a forest or into some uncharted land, tell someone where you are going and give them a copy of your itinerary. Carry a phone to call for help if necessary. Keep track of time. Bring a compass. Wear sturdy walking shoes and appropriate clothing. Carry nutritious snacks and plenty of water.

When you know what plants are native to your area, you can better engage in wildcrafting and further explore your connection to the natural energies where you live.

In the following sections you'll find a set of common correspondences for various natural energies. I've chosen to classify plant matter as trees, flowers, and herbs. At the end of the chapter there is also a reference for stones, as these are also of the earth.

> IMPORTANT: Although I occasionally include traditional medicinal herbal lore as additional information, if you are interested in using herbs as medical or therapeutic supplements, you must refer to a reliable medicinal guide. Both John Lust's *The Herb Book* and Christopher Hobbs's *Herbal Remedies for Dummies* are good resources.

The Magic of Trees

Trees are the pillars of our world. They anchor our ground and seem to hold up the sky. They form the backbone of the green witch's practice. While we tend to focus on herbs, we also work with wood, often when something more physically stable or permanent is required. The green witch's staff and stang, for example, are made of wood, as is the more traditional witch's tool, the wand. Sticks and twigs form the basis of many protective amulets, as do rounds cut from the cross-section of branches and inscribed with symbols. Trees also have many practical uses, such as supporting plants and serving as natural fences. Wood is also used to build homes and furniture.

Following are sixteen trees of use to the green witch, plus some associated lore. These trees grow in various areas of North America. The parts of trees used include bark, leaves, and inner wood.

BIRCH (*BETULA SPP.*)

The traditional witch's broom is made of birch twigs. Magically, birch is associated with cleansing, protection, and purification. It is also associated with children; cradles were often made of birch wood.

OAK (*QUERCUS ROBUR*)

Oak is one of those traditional woods that are firmly entrenched in folklore; it is magically associated with defense, thunder, strength, courage, healing, longevity, protection, and good fortune. Because the wood is very strong and durable and possesses a certain reputation for indestructibility, oak has been used in home construction and in shipbuilding. The bark is used to tan leather and as a dye. Acorns, the fruit of the oak tree, are symbols of fertility. When found growing in oak trees, mistletoe was considered to be particularly potent by the druids and important in their magical work.

MAPLE (*ACER SPP.*)

Maple is another popular tree used for cabinetry and by artisans. It is also a source of dye and maple sugar. Magically, maple is used for love, prosperity, life and health, and general abundance.

PINE (*PINUS SPP.*)

Commonly used in building and construction, the pine is one of the most widely found trees in North America. Its resin is used for the creation of turpentine and soaps, and the production of rosin. Amber, one of the most beloved gems for magical jewelry, is fossilized pine sap. Pine oil, another product of the pine tree, is commonly added to household cleansing products, proof that the scent is associated with a sense of purification. Magically, pine is used for cleansing and purification, healing, clarity of mind, prosperity, and protection from evil.

CEDAR (*THUJA OCCIDENTALIS*—WHITE CEDAR; *CUPRESSUS NOOTKATENSIS*—YELLOW CEDAR; *JUNIPERUS VIRGINIANA*—RED CEDAR)

Another precious wood that is recognized by many cultures as magical and powerful, cedar has been known throughout the ages for its protective qualities as well as its ability to repel insects and pests. With its aromatic scent, cedar was often given as an offering. Yellow cedar, found in North America, grows in a roughly conical shape and is often used in hedges. The other kind of cedar found in North America is the red cedar (*Juniperus virginiana*). Magically, cedar is associated with healing, spirituality, purification, protection, prosperity, and harmony.

ROWAN (*PYRUS AUCUPARIA, SORBUS AUCUPARIA*)

Rowan is also known as quicken, hornbeam, witchwood, and mountain ash (although it is technically not a true ash, it is so called due to the similarity of the leaves). Rowan berries have been used in brewing and the bark has been used for tanning and as a dye. Curiously, rowan is said to be either a favorite of witches and fairies or anathema to them. Magical associations include improving psychic powers, divination, healing, protection from evil, peace, creativity, success, and change and transformation.

POPLAR (*POPULUS SPP.*)

Also known as aspen, poplar's magical associations include prosperity, communication, exorcism, and purification.

ASH (*FRAXINUS EXCELSIOR*)

Ash is one of the trees considered by some European cultures to be the World Tree. Magically, ash is associated with water, strength, intellect, willpower, protection, justice, balance and harmony, skill, travel, weather, and wisdom.

WILLOW (SALIX ALBA)

The white willow, also known as the weeping willow, has long flexible branches that are woven into what we know as wicker-work. Long associated with the moon, the willow has a great affinity for water and is often found growing near it. In folklore, the willow is associated with the Goddess and feminine cycles. Thanks to the ability of cuttings to easily and quickly recover from trauma, willow is also associated with growth and renewal. Magical associations of willow include love, tranquility, harmony, protection, and healing.

WITCH HAZEL (HAMAMELIS VIRGINIANA)

Also known as snapping hazelnut, for the spontaneous cracking open of its seedpods, witch hazel has long been used as a poultice for bruises and swellings. Witch hazel extracts are used for their astringent properties. Magical associations include protection, healing, and peace.

HONEYSUCKLE (LONICERA CAPRIFOLIUM, LONICERA PERICLYMENUM)

Also known as woodbine or hedge-tree, the honeysuckle is associated with liminal or transitional states. The scent of honeysuckle flowers is strongest in the evening. Magical associations include psychic awareness, harmony, healing, prosperity, and happiness.

APPLE (PYRUS MALUS)

Apple trees are found all over the Northern Hemisphere. Their widespread availability and fertile abundance bring to mind their association with life, longevity, and fertility. The fruit is used in cooking, baking, and brewing. Folklore associates the apple with the afterlife, fairies, creativity, and the otherworld. Magically, apples and apple trees are associated with love, healing, harmony, and longevity.

ELDER (SAMBUCUS CANADENSIS, SAMBUCUS NIGRA)

Elder is also known as witchwood. It is said that bad luck will fall upon anyone who does not ask the tree's permission three times before harvesting any part of it. Folklore associates the elder with the crone aspect of the Goddess and with witches, and thus elder wood is rarely used to make furniture or as firewood for fear of incurring their wrath. Medicinally, elder bark is used as a diuretic, purgative, and emetic. The berries are used as a laxative and diuretic and also induce perspiration, and the leaves are used as an external emollient for irritated skin, sprains, and bruises. An infusion of elderflowers taken as a tea encourages the body to perspire, thus helping the body to work through a cold or illness, and also helps loosen chest and sinus congestion. Elderflower water makes an excellent topical application for irritated skin, including problems such as sunburn and acne, as well as an eyewash. Magically, elder wood is associated with protection (especially against being struck by lightning), prosperity, and healing.

YEW (TAXUS BACCATA)

Yew is poisonous, which may be one of the reasons it is so closely associated with death. It is a European tree that figures largely in the lore of witchcraft and natural magic. The yew produces a very hard wood and was used where construction required an unyielding, inflexible structure. Magically, it is associated with spirits and the otherworld.

HAWTHORN (*CRATAEGUS OXYACANTHA*)

Also known as may tree, mayflower, thorn, whitethorn, and haw, the hawthorn shrub was often used as a boundary marker. In fact, "haw" is an old word for hedge. Hawthorn is a magical tree. If it grows together with an oak and ash tree, it is said that the fairy folk can be seen among the trees. Even where it grows alone, hawthorn is considered to be a fairy favorite. Like oak, the hawthorn produces hard wood and great heat when burned. Magical associations include fertility, harmony, happiness, the otherworld, and protection.

HAZEL (*CORYLUS AVELLANA*)

The hazel tree has long been associated in European folklore with wisdom. Gods and mythological figures associated with the hazel include Thor, Brigid, and Apollo. The nuts and branches are used for magic, and the hazel is associated with luck, fertility, protection, and wish granting.

TREE ATTUNEMENT EXERCISE

Before you begin, refresh your memory on sensing energy techniques in Chapter 3.

1. Pick a tree. Stand next to it. Hold one hand about 1 inch away from the bark. Extend your awareness and feel the energy of the tree. After you've finished this exercise, make notes in your journal.

2. With the same tree, touch the bark. Explore how the tree feels to your hands. Bend close and smell the tree. Close your eyes and listen to the sounds the tree makes in response to the environment. Look closely at the tree and see the different textures, colors, and markings. If it has fruit and you know it to be safe, taste it. Make notes in your journal.

3. Conduct these exercises with different kinds of trees. Compare and contrast your experiences.

4. Do these exercises with different trees of the same genus. What are the similarities between the trees? What are the differences?

COLLECTING AND USING WOOD

Some people have difficulty with the idea of cutting live wood away from a tree or bush because they don't know how to do it properly. When you use fresh wood, you capture a lot of life and energy, which may be exactly what you're looking for in your ritual work or any practice that will involve this wood. Deadfall is wood the tree has discarded as no longer useful. This may not be the kind of vibrant, living energy you're looking for. It depends on your personal view of working with the world of nature. If you cut fresh wood, you'll likely have to let it dry, as sap and juices can gum up your saw and sandpaper.

So why use fresh wood? The answer is simple: your magical intent is implemented as soon as you choose the tree from which you are going to cut some wood. By selecting the tree, you are presenting your request to the energy of the tree itself. As you cut, you're focusing on your goal. From the very first move, you're empowering it in conjunction with the tree, if it has agreed to donate its wood to your cause.

How do you ask the tree for help? Put your hands on the tree and present your intention to it, speaking either aloud or in your mind. Think through why you need the wood, exactly how it will be used, and for what goal. All these thoughts and feelings will flow through your energy into the energy of the tree. Then wait. Trees often need a bit of time to absorb your request, for they function at a different rate than we do. Sometimes the tree will accept your request right away, though at other times, you may not get a prompt sense of acceptance or denial. In that case, thank the tree for its time, and tell it you will return in a day or two. When you come back, place your hands on the tree again and reach out with your energy. Restate your need and wait for an answer. Sometimes all the tree needs is time.

The tree won't tell you in words, of course, if it's all right to cut its branches. Instead, you'll gain a sense of peace or agreement. Or, alternatively, you may get a sense of maybe this isn't such a good idea. In that case, thank the tree again for its time and consideration, wish it well, and find another tree to ask.

Tap Into the Energies of Flowers

Flowers are the pretty parts of plants that carry valuable and essential reproductive information. Technically, they constitute part of an herb, shrub, or tree, but they are separated here because we often think of the flower as the identifying aspect of a plant. Also, in natural magic, the flower itself is often the part used.

Flowers can be dried whole to be used in wreaths or arrangements or pressed and used in a magical collage or in potpourri. When dried, flowers can also be crumbled and used in herbal blends for such things as teas, sachets, and sprinkling powders.

The flower of a plant carries a tidy bundle of energy, for it is the sexual organ of the plant, how the plant reproduces. Do dried flowers carry a different energy than fresh flowers do? Yes and no; the intrinsic energy remains, but its expression is different. For certain rituals or charms you may want the vibrancy of fresh flowers, whereas for other charms, such as sachets or powders, you may prefer dried flowers, which tend to exhibit a slower, longer-lasting energy.

Here are nineteen flowers commonly found in a green witch's garden. They are also used magically.

CARNATION (*DIANTHUS SPP.*)

Also known as gillyflower, the carnation has a wonderful healing energy and makes an excellent gift for the sick. Carnations are used magically for protection, strength, energy, luck, and healing.

DAFFODIL (*NARCISSUS SPP.*)

Also known as narcissus and asphodel, the daffodil is an excellent flower to use in charms for love and charms for fertility. Magically, the daffodil is associated with luck, fertility, and love.

DAISY (*CHRYSANTHEMUM LEUCANTHEMUM*)

Also known as field daisy and the eye of the day, the daisy is commonly associated with love and flirtation. We have all plucked the petals from a daisy—"he loves me, he loves me not." Magically, the daisy is associated with love, hope, and innocence. Use the daisy in magic associated with children as well.

GARDENIA (*GARDENIA SPP.*)

Gardenia is an excellent flower that attracts tranquil energy to a place or individual. Adding gardenia petals to a healing sachet or using them in a healing ritual incorporates this tranquil energy and helps the healing move at a controlled pace. Gardenia is also commonly used in love spells and charms. Magically, gardenia is associated with harmony, healing, love, and peace.

GERANIUM (*PELARGONIUM SPP.*)

Grown indoors or out, geraniums carry strong protective energy and extend this energy through the area around them. Red geraniums have traditionally been associated with protection. Rose geranium is used in love spells. Magically, geraniums are associated with fertility, love, healing, courage, and protection.

HYACINTH (MUSCARI RACEMOSUM, HYACINTHUS NON-SCRIPTUS)

Both grape and wild hyacinths have a lovely springlike scent. The perennial wild hyacinth, also known as the bluebell, is smaller and daintier than the cultivated grape hyacinth. Hyacinths bloom for only a short period of time, but in that short period produce a vibrant energy. Hyacinths are named for the youth of Greek legend, beloved of Apollo, whose accidental death Apollo commemorated by creating the flower. Hyacinths are magically associated with love, happiness, and protection.

IRIS (IRIS FLORENTINA)

Also known as flags, the iris is a lovely spring flower magically used for purification and blessing as well as wisdom. The three petals are said to symbolize faith, wisdom, and valor. The root is called orris root, and when ground up it produces a mildly sweet powder used as a scent fixative in potpourri. Orris powder is also used for peace, harmony, and love.

JASMINE (JASMINUM SPP.)

Also known as jessamine, jasmine possesses a heady but delicate scent that is usually stronger at night. Because of this, it is often associated with the moon and feminine energy. Jasmine, which has long been associated with seduction and sensuality, is a perfumer's prized ingredient. Magically, jasmine is associated with love, meditation, spirituality, harmony, and prosperity.

LAVENDER (*LAVANDULA SPP.*)

Another perennial favorite, lavender is used frequently in magical and nonmagical applications. Thanks to its gentle scent, it is an ideal herb to use in conjunction with magic for children, for it encourages relaxation and sleep. Magically, lavender is associated with peace, harmony, tranquility, love, purification, and healing.

LILAC (*SYRINGA VULGARIS*)

The sweet, wild scent of lilacs in late spring is a heady experience. The flowers of this shrub are usually white or shades of purple. Magically, they are used for protection and banishing negative energy.

LILY (*LILIUM SPP.*)

The lily family is very large. In general, lilies are associated with protection and the elimination of hexes. Day lilies bring to mind the concept of cycles. In some cultures, lilies are associated with the concept of death and the afterlife, supporting the association with rebirth and cycles.

LILY OF THE VALLEY (*CONVALLARIA MAGALIS*)

This tiny cascade of white or cream-colored bell-shaped flowers has a delicate scent. Magically, it enhances concentration and mental ability and is used to encourage happiness.

PANSY (*VIOLA TRICOLOR*)

Also known as love-in-idleness and Johnny-jump-up, the pansy is a hardy, cheerful-looking plant with multicolored flowers related to the violet. It blooms throughout the summer and comes in both annual and perennial varieties. Magically, it is used for divination, communication, happiness, and love.

POPPY (*PAPAVER RHOEAS*)

Also known as the corn poppy, the red poppy is a bright flower with a furry green stem and leaves. Although the red poppy (*Papaver rhoeas*) is a gentle narcotic in large quantities, it is the *Papaver somniferum* species of poppies that is toxic and the source of opium. Poppy seeds are used in cooking and baking, and sometimes oil is extracted to be used in cooking as well. Magically, the poppy is associated with tranquility, fertility, prosperity, love, sleep, and invisibility.

ROSE (*ROSA SPP.*)

Across cultures and throughout history, the rose is one of the most famous flowers. Its scent is unmistakable. Folklore and literature have made the rose synonymous with love, although that is far from being the only association it carries. Roses create an atmosphere of beauty that encourages closeness with nature. The rose is a very feminine flower and is edible if unsprayed and prepared correctly (see Chapter 9 for recipes using roses and other flowers). The real flower has a gentle scent; it is unfortunate that artificially scented rose products are heavy and overly sweet. Magically, the rose is associated with healing, divination, tranquility, harmony, psychic ability, spirituality, and protection.

SNAPDRAGON (*ANTIRRHINUM MAJUS*)

Snapdragons have a lovely innocent energy. Magically, they are used for protection, particularly from illusion or deception, or to reflect negative energy to its source. Plant snapdragons along the perimeter of your garden to protect it.

SUNFLOWER (*HELIANTHUS SPP.*)

Also known as Peruvian marigold, the sunflower is, of course, associated with the sun and its energy, which means it carries magical associations of happiness, success, and health. The sunflower is also associated with welcome and family. The plant's abundant seeds carry the magical associations of fertility. Sunflowers are excellent in a celebration ritual or during a summer solstice ritual. Germinate the seeds and then plant them to increase the energy of abundance in your garden in general. (Be sure you choose specific seeds meant for planting instead of planting random seeds, so you will know what size of sunflower to expect!)

TULIP (*TULIPA SPP.*)

The chalice or cuplike shape of the tulip makes this flower ideal for use for prosperity and abundance magic. The tulip is also associated with protection, love, and happiness.

VIOLET (*VIOLA ODORATA*)

Also known as sweet violet, the violet is a delicate flower used for peace, hope, harmony, protection, luck, love, sleep, and tranquility. Use violet in charms and sachets designed to maintain tranquility and to encourage peace, particularly among people. Combine violet with lavender for a child's herbal pillow to aid sleep and calm nightmares. Violet also has aspects of fertility and abundance, which are reflected in how easily the plant propagates itself.

Potent Herbs and Greens

Generally, a plant referred to as an herb possesses some sort of medicinal, culinary, or magical value. Botanists and gardeners sometimes differentiate herbs from other plants by the stem: if the plant has a "woody" stem above the ground, it's not an herb but a tree or a shrub. According to this definition, mint is an herb, but rosemary is not.

In the magical and spiritual world, however, the term "herb" is used as a catchall for the bits of trees, flowers, spices, and all sorts of plants. Herbs thus form a huge portion of the green witch's practice. Following the herbs, you'll find some miscellaneous greens that are also useful (though often overlooked).

The following list comprises some aromatic and culinary herbs.

ALLSPICE (*PIMENTA OFFICINALIS*)

Also known as pimento or Jamaica pepper, the dried allspice berry is a common staple in the kitchen spice rack. Called "allspice" because it incorporates flavors such as clove, cinnamon, and pepper, it is a common flavoring for spice cookies. The sweet yet spicy aroma is released when the dried berry is crushed. Allspice berries make wonderful additions to prosperity blends and any magic focusing on increasing energy, love, healing, and luck.

ANGELICA (*ANGELICA ARCHANGELICA*)

Also known as archangel or angel's herb, this fragrant plant has been used throughout the centuries for improving digestion, flavoring wines and liqueurs, and making candy. Magically, it is particularly powerful when used for protection and purification.

BASIL (*OCIMUM BASILICUM*)

Also known as sweet basil and St. Joseph's Wort, basil is commonly found in spice racks and in kitchen gardens all over Europe and the Americas. It is extremely versatile in the culinary arts and is an excellent all-purpose magical herb as well. Basil is used for prosperity, success, peace, protection, happiness, purification, tranquility, and love.

BAY (*LAURUS NOBILIS*)

Also known as sweet bay and sweet laurel, bay was used to crown the victor of games in ancient Greece and Rome. Bay is magically associated with success, wisdom, and divination. Write a wish on a bay leaf and burn it, or sleep with it under your pillow for dreams that offer some sort of guidance as to how to pursue your goal. (If you burn the bay leaf, make sure your area is well ventilated, for the smoke can be mildly hallucinogenic.)

CHAMOMILE (*CHAMAEMELUM NOBILE, MATRICARIA RECUTITA*)

Also known as manzanilla, chamomile (both the Roman and German varieties) is another versatile popular magical and medicinal herb. It is excellent for soothing stomach problems, headaches, and nerves and is an ideal herb to give to children. Magically, it is used for prosperity, peace, healing, harmony, and happiness.

CALENDULA (*CALENDULA OFFICINALIS*)

Although sometimes identified as the pot marigold, calendula is not the common marigold (*Tagetes spp.*). Calendula is edible, whereas the garden marigold is not. Calendula has been used medicinally to treat skin irritations, such as eczema, bruises, scars, and scrapes. Magically, it is used for happiness, prosperity, love, psychic powers, and harmony.

CINNAMON (*CINNAMOMUM SPP.*)

Cinnamon is one of the must-have multipurpose herbs in a green witch's stock. It possesses a great amount of energy, and a pinch can be added to anything to rev up the power level. It is also excellent for spells and charms involving money. Magically, cinnamon is associated

with success, action, healing, protection, energy, love, prosperity, and
purification.

CARAWAY (CARUM CARVI)

The seed of the caraway plant is excellent to use for protection
against negativity. It's also a good antitheft herb, so add some to the
garden sachets you place outdoors to keep little animal intruders from
nibbling at your plants, as well as in protective sachets or charms
in your home. Magical associations include health, mental abilities,
protection, fidelity, and antitheft.

CLOVE (SYZYGIUM AROMATICUM)

The small dried bud of the clove plant is used in cooking, baking,
and magic. Magically, clove is associated with protection, purification,
mental ability, and healing. Add three cloves to a sachet or charm to
tie in protective and purifying energy to keep the charm's action pure
and focused for a longer period of time. A sachet of rosemary, angelica,
sage, three cloves, and a pinch of salt tied shut with red thread or
ribbon is a good all-purpose sachet to hang above a door or in your car
to turn away negativity and protect the area.

COMFREY (SYMPHYTUM OFFICINALE)

Also known as boneset or knitbone, comfrey is renowned as a
healing herb. Magically, it is associated with health, healing, protection
during travel, and prosperity.

DILL (ANETHUM GRAVEOLENS)

Also known as dillweed, dill comes in two forms: seed and weed,
which is the feathery dried leaves of the plant. Either may be used in

green witch work. Dill is magically used for good fortune, tranquility, prosperity, lust, and protection.

GINGER (*ZINGIBER OFFICINALE*)

Wild or cultivated, gingerroot is an ideal herb to add to rituals and spells because it acts like a booster for the power involved. Like the energy of cinnamon, the heat of the ginger revs up the energy associated with your work. Ginger can also be used to jump-start love, stimulate finances, and increase the potential for success in just about anything. Medicinally, it is used for fighting colds, calming the stomach, and suppressing nausea.

MARJORAM (*ORIGANUM MAJORANA*)

Also known as winter sweet, marjoram is similar to oregano, but sweeter and milder. Marjoram was used by the ancient Greeks to crown newly married couples. It is used for happiness, protection, love, and joy, particularly in family environments. (Oregano [*Origanum vulgare*], a similar herb, is used for love, courage, and action.)

MINT (*MENTHA SPP.*)

There is a wide variety of green or garden mints, which are versatile herbs to grow in a garden or on the kitchen windowsill. An infusion of the leaves will help ease most headaches, stimulate the appetite, and aid digestion. Magical associations are prosperity, joy, fertility, purification, love, and success.

MUGWORT (*ARTEMISIA VULGARIS*)

Also known as artemisia and sailor's tobacco, mugwort is another ubiquitous witchy herb. A decoction of the leaves is said to help open your mind before you try divination. Magically, it is associated with prophetic dreams and divination, relaxation and tranquility, protection, banishing, and consecration.

NUTMEG (MYRISTICA FRAGRANS)

Medicinally, nutmeg quells nausea and soothes digestive problems (although it can be toxic in large doses). Magically, it is associated with psychic abilities, happiness, love, money, and health.

PARSLEY (PETROSELINUM CRISPUM)

In ancient Greece, parsley was used for such varied purposes as sprinkling on corpses to neutralize the smell of decay and making victors' crowns to celebrate success. It is magically associated with power, strength, lust, purification, and prosperity. Both the seeds and the leaves can be used.

ROSEMARY (ROSMARINUS OFFICINALIS)

Practical applications of rosemary include use as a skin tonic applied externally and as a hair rinse to add shine to dark hair and soothe itchy scalp. An infusion taken as a tea will help ease a headache. Magical associations include protection, improving memory, wisdom, health, and healing.

SAGE (SALVIA SPP.)

Sage is perhaps the herb most commonly used for purification and protection. An infusion taken as a tea will help settle a sour stomach and ease digestion and can help calm anxiety as well. Magical associations include purification and protection, wisdom, health, and long life.

VERBENA (VERBENA OFFICINALIS, VERBENA SPP.)

Also known as vervain, enchanter's herb, herb of grace, and van van, verbena is an excellent all-purpose herb. Medicinally, an infusion of verbena helps calm headaches, eases stress, and makes a relaxing bedtime tea. Magically versatile, verbena is associated with divination, protection, inspiration, abundance, love, peace, tranquility, healing, prosperity, skill in artistic performance, and the reversal of negative activity. Make a verbena oil by infusing the fresh plant in a light olive oil or grapeseed oil to use as a standard blessing/protection oil. Add crumbled verbena leaves to any sachet to round out the positive energies you are drawing together. It is an excellent all-purpose herb to add to any charm bag or spell to encourage success.

YARROW (ACHILLEA MILLEFOLIUM)

Also known as milfoil, millefeuille, yarroway, or bloodwort, yarrow is a common garden herb grown for its attractive silvery foliage. The leaves and stem of yarrow, harvested in late summer, have traditionally been used as a poultice to staunch blood. Magically, it is used for courage, healing, and love.

MOSS

Moss is a type of plant that is the first to grow in a seemingly barren area. It's also tenacious and survives in the oddest places where you wouldn't think anything could grow. Moss prefers a humid, shady environment, and can and will grow on trees, rocks, dead wood, and soil—anywhere there may be a small crack or gap where particles of soil can collect. It can grow with no apparent place to root whatsoever, which is possible because moss technically does not have roots. Moss absorbs water through its leaves. Because it survives with little maintenance and in improbable locations, moss is associated with perseverance, patience, nurturing, and grounding. Because it is lush even in seemingly inhospitable areas, it's also associated with serenity and calm.

FERNS

Ferns are lovely ethereal plants that range from fragile to remarkably sturdy. They grow in a variety of climates and settings, depending on the genus and species. They're often associated with invisibility, love, chastity, protection from evil, and unlocking doors.

GRASS

Grass is so common that most green witches overlook it. Grass isn't found only on our lawns; it's also found tall and waving by the roadside or growing through cracks in alleyways or vacant lots. Like moss, it is associated with serenity. Grass also has a quirky humor: if you want it to grow, it will resist, whereas if you try to get rid of it, it will keep popping up. Grass is a trickster. It's also highly adaptable.

Using Stones: The Bones of the Earth

Although they're not usually thought of as growing things like plants and trees, stones are sometimes referred to as "the bones of the earth." Small, nonperishable, and convenient, stones and crystals constitute a very useful element of the green witch's practice. Don't overlook working with gems and crystals simply because they don't pop up in your back garden like regular granite and clay do.

Stones have multiple uses in green magic. They can be empowered on their own and carried or left in specific areas. They can also be worn as jewelry, added to potpourris and herbal blends, powdered and added to incenses, added whole to incenses while they mature (but remove them before you burn the incense), added to oils, tucked into potted plants, and buried. The possibilities are endless.

Here are twenty stones of use to the green witch:

Moss Agate

Moss agate is used for healing, for calm, and for stress relief. Moss agate looks like strands of moss caught in ice or in a translucent, blurry crystal. Like most green stones, it is associated with nature.

Tree Agate

Tree agate is much like moss agate, except instead of looking like strands of green caught in translucent crystal, it looks like strands of green twining through an opaque white stone.

Amethyst

Amethyst is purple quartz and is associated with psychic power, truth, balance, protection, and healing.

Aventurine

Aventurine is a green opaque stone with tiny flecks of gold in it. It is associated with luck, prosperity, and health.

Bloodstone

Bloodstone is a green opaque stone with flecks of red in it. Magically, it is associated with health (especially of the blood) and protection.

Carnelian

Carnelian is a milky orange stone. Magically, it is associated with success and manifestation.

Citrine

Citrine is yellow quartz and often appears as yellow ice or is yellow and white. It is found in points and as a tumbled stone. It works to calm nightmares, aids in digestion, focuses the mind, and enhances creativity.

HEMATITE

Hematite is a dull silver-colored stone (it can also show up as black, brown, and reddish-brown). In the Middle Ages, it was called a bloodstone, so if you come across a reference to a bloodstone make sure you know which stone is being referred to. Hematite has iron in it and magically is associated with grounding excess or unbalanced energy. It also deflects negativity and is thus associated with defense, healing, and justice.

JADE

Usually green, this stone is associated with wisdom, prosperity, fertility, health, and protection.

JASPER

Found in many colors, jasper is most commonly red. It is good for grounding and stabilizing energy and for protection and courage. Bury jaspers in the four corners of your garden to deepen its connection to the earth and secure its energy for more balanced growth and yield.

LAPIS LAZULI

A deep blue stone with flecks of gold, lapis lazuli is associated with leadership, communication, stress relief, creativity, joy, and harmony.

MALACHITE

A deep green stone with bands or circles of lighter green, malachite is associated with fertility and earth mysteries. Malachite is a wonderful stone for green witches to work with, for it helps strengthen your connection to the world of nature. Try carrying or wearing a piece of malachite while you communicate with the world of green, whether you are tramping through a field or digging in your backyard. See how it affects your work and your perceptions.

MOONSTONE

A milky white stone, sometimes with overtones of green, peach, or gray, the moonstone is magically associated with protection during travel, children, love, and peace. It also has a connection to the Goddess.

QUARTZ (CLEAR)

An easily obtained stone, a clear quartz crystal looks like ice, often with small inclusions (which do not affect the stone's energy at all). Quartz crystal amplifies energy, stores power, enhances psychic ability, and absorbs negativity. It has become immensely popular and can be found in tumbled form and in point form (which is how it grows) and is often set in jewelry. Quartz crystal is an excellent all-purpose stone to work with.

QUARTZ (ROSE)

Another common stone, rose quartz looks like pink ice. Like other quartz crystals, rose quartz amplifies and stores energy. Rose quartz is specifically used to boost self-esteem and encourage self-love, for emotional healing, to foster affection, and to transform negative energy into positive, supportive energy.

QUARTZ (SMOKY)

Smoky quartz is a gray quartz used for grounding and to clear obstacles. It strengthens intuition and helps manifest thought into action, goals into reality.

SNOWFLAKE OBSIDIAN

An opaque black stone with spots that look like white or pale gray snowflakes, this stone is used for protection. Regular obsidian, which is all black, is also used for protection. I prefer to use snowflake obsidian in green witch work, as it reminds me of winter and midnight, two important parts of the natural cycle of days and seasons.

SODALITE

A dark blue stone with white or gray veins, sodalite is used for balancing emotions and enhancing wisdom.

TIGER'S EYE

A glossy, satiny, brown stone with bands of satiny dark gold, the tiger's eye is used for strength, courage, luck, and prosperity.

TURQUOISE

A pale blue stone with fine black or gray lines running through it, turquoise is an excellent children's stone, for it protects and strengthens gently. It also helps focus the mind and will.

CLEANSING STONES

Before you use a stone, it is important to cleanse and purify it. Cleansing is a physical removal of dirt or debris; just wash the stone in plain water and scrub it with a cloth or brush if necessary. Purifying the stone means cleaning its energy. Before you use a stone for any magical purpose, it should always be purified.

There are several ways to purify a stone:

- Leave it in sunlight or moonlight for a specific period of time.
- Bury it in a small dish of salt for one to three days. Salt is a natural purifier. Never use salt to cleanse a stone that has iron in it, such as hematite, or if it is set in metal, for the metal will rust.
- Bury it in a small dish of dirt for a measured period of time. Earth will accomplish the same purpose in the same way that salt does, though it may take longer.

- Immerse the stone in water for a measured period of time. Moving water will purify it faster, although leaving the stone in a small bowl of water for a longer period will work as well. You can add a small pinch of salt to the dish of water to speed the process, unless you are cleansing a stone set in metal or a stone with iron content, such as hematite.

How long you leave the stone to purify by your chosen method depends on how much foreign energy is clinging to it (see the following).

ATTUNING TO STONES

Before you use a stone for a magical purpose, get to know its particular energy so that when you test its energy later on, you have an idea of how much purification it requires.

When you first bring a stone home from a rock shop or from the great outdoors, cleanse and purify it using one of the previous methods for one full week to ensure that it has been completely cleared of any foreign energy. Don't worry; you cannot remove the innate energy of an object, so it's impossible to overpurify.

When the week is up, prepare yourself by finding a quiet space and settling down with the stone and your green witch notebook. Take three deep breaths, releasing tension and focusing on the stone in your hand with each exhalation. Begin by testing the energy of the stone by using one of the energy-sensing methods given in Chapter 3. How does the stone's energy feel to you? Make as many observations and associations as you can. Remember to write them down. What is important is that you are making personal observations about the energy, not that you hit on the same correspondences that are traditionally associated with the stone.

Once you have an idea of how the energy of the stone feels to you while it is completely natural and unaffected by any other energy, you will be able to evaluate the stone before any future use to determine how much purification it will need. Everyone senses energy in a different way, but perhaps the stone will feel particularly heavy or negative to you, or you will gain a sense of wrongness, or simply a difference from what you expect to feel when you next pick it up to use it. If the stone feels drastically different, purify the stone for a longer period of time. If you have used the stone for a previous magical purpose, it is important to purify it, even if it was for the same intention, for as the stone is used it can collect other energies. As you become more experienced in sensing energy, you will be able to identify how much purification a stone needs by comparing its current energy with what you know its base natural energy is.

EMPOWERING STONES

To prepare a stone for magical use once it has been purified, you must program or empower it. This step aligns the stone's natural energy with your magical intention. While the stone's natural energies will function even if you do not empower it with your magical intention, they will function in accordance to your desire much more efficiently if you program it with your precise need and magical goal.

- To program a stone with your intention, hold it between your palms. Close your eyes and take three deep breaths, centering yourself and focusing on your magical goal.

- Visualize your goal as already achieved, which means you should take a minute or two to daydream about how terrific you'll feel once the situation is the way you want it.

- Now visualize a sparkling light forming around your hands. This sparkling light is the energy summoned from within you to empower the stone. It is energy programmed with your magical goal. Imagine the sparkling light being absorbed into the stone.

- At this point, say aloud what your goal is and what the stone is to be used for. For example, you may say, "This stone brings me prosperity," if you are programming it for financial success or abundance. Some people find it easier to repeat a phrase like this over and over in order to raise and focus the energy upon what they are empowering. I tend to be a very quiet green witch, so I quietly whisper my chosen phrase over and over until the words become a stream of sound. I visualize that sound being directed into the stone.

- Once the energy has been absorbed into the stone, the stone has been programmed with your magical intention and empowered for that use.

Chapter 6

Keep a Green Witch Garden

THE GARDEN IS AN IMPORTANT ELEMENT of the green witch's practice. Working with nature does not always mean immersing yourself in the great outdoors. As many modern green witches are discovering, both out of necessity and in their desire to adapt to the needs of the modern world, there are many other methods of interacting with nature's energy. Creative solutions are required in urban areas. This chapter looks at how the concept of the garden functions in the modern, urban green witch's reality.

The wilderness is not the antithesis of civilization. The two are environmental extremes that complement each other. People require a secure environment in order to function well, and so over the millennia we have carved out sections of the wilderness and organized them. The city is not evil, and the wilderness is not automatically good. Because the modern urban green witch understands this, part of her calling involves bridging the gap between "wild" and "civilized."

There will always be some products you will not be able to grow where you live. Not many people in North America, for example, can grow cinnamon. You don't have to break your back and your budget trying to forge a personal energetic connection with highly exotic plants that won't grow where you live. Do what you can, when you can. Growing plants whose energy you can work with offers you a more than adequate opportunity for a deeper dialogue experience and interaction with nature.

The Power in a Garden

The practice of green witchcraft is innately tied to the agricultural cycle, which dictated the rhythm of the lives of our ancestors. The agricultural societies of yesteryear focused on the seasonal changes of soil and crops. Witchcraft's concern with fertility, sowing, tending, and reaping (metaphorically and otherwise) is rooted in that agricultural tradition.

It thus makes a certain kind of sense that the green witch has a strong spiritual and personal connection to nature and the land. The connection to nature is also a practical one. The witch's garden provides a ready source of food as well as components of spells and ingredients for various remedies.

By working with a garden, indoors or out, the green witch is interacting with nature on a personal basis. Hands-on practice offers you the opportunity to physically feel your connection to nature. It gives you the simple pleasure of working in harmony with the natural cycle.

Working with a garden of any kind also allows you to meditate on the concept of harmony and balance in a completely different way. There is a very real give-and-take of energy involved in tending a garden. The time and care you put into maintaining the garden is directly reflected in the garden's health and what you harvest. Like a person, a garden is also in a constant state of change. Just as you solve one problem in your life and another pops up, what you do to tend your garden one week may be different from what you do the next week. The sun may beat down without mercy for weeks, drying your precious plants to a crisp, only to be followed by a monsoon-like week of pouring rain that nearly drowns what you've managed to salvage. Working with a garden is a continuous lesson in patience, acceptance, and recognition that nature functions as an independent system that operates no matter what we humans do.

THE HARVEST FROM THE GREEN WITCH'S GARDEN

Are herbs you buy less powerful than those you grow? Are the spices you use off your kitchen shelf any less powerful than those from your garden? It depends on who you ask. Hands-on work allows a green witch to understand the energy and power of a plant from seed to dried form. However, even the ground spices on your spice rack originally came from a natural source. Being practical, the green witch uses what she has on hand. You don't have to harvest the plant yourself in order to use its energy. You can reach out and touch the energy of the herb and make a personal connection with purchased herbs. If you want something that isn't local, you can buy it from an herbalist, a metaphysical supply shop, or online. If you buy herbs from one of these sources, however, be sure to use them only for magical purposes; don't be tempted to make tea unless the purchased herb is certified as being safe for internal consumption.

A gardening climate zone map can be an immense help to you as you plan your garden. Climate zones are determined by maximum and minimum temperatures, which in turn determine what plants can thrive in the area. You can see the USDA National Plant Hardiness Zone Map on the United States National Arboretum web page, the introduction to which can be found at: www.usna.usda.gov/Hardzone/index.html.

As for fresh versus dried, the energy is similar, though in different forms. Think of the energy of a live plant as running water, whereas the dried herb's energy might be like the water in a cup. As long as the plant is alive, its energy flows. Once harvested, the energy of the plant is like water caught in a container. It continues being water, and it has the energy of the water, but the energy is still instead of flowing. What you need to do with the energy of a plant or herb and where and how you need to do your work will help you determine whether to use fresh or dried. Using fresh plant matter in a sachet, for example, isn't a good idea because the fresh leaves will mold and rot.

Designing Your Garden

The urban green witch faces several challenges when it comes to gardening and creating a personal space in which to commune with nature. In a city or suburb, many people do not have an ideal space in which to lay out a garden. If you don't have a strip of earth somewhere along the path to your front door, or if you're bound to an apartment and have no land at all, you may be surprised to find out that you in fact have several options. Check with your city hall or environmental division to see if your city sponsors public garden space. You can apply for one of these garden plots, which are usually fenced off and protected, often for free or at a low rental cost. You may have to travel to it, but you can grow whatever you like within legal parameters.

If you prefer something closer to home, you can create a balcony or window garden. The container garden is the green witch's answer to the challenge of limited space and high-rise or apartment living. One of the wonderful things about container gardening on a balcony or in a window is that if the containers or the plants themselves are small enough to move easily, you can always change your arrangement.

> Keep notes in your journal on what plants respond well to the lighting and environment of your chosen garden space. Also keep notes on the evolution of your garden over the seasons. Next year, you can create a more successful garden or experiment with something completely new.

Your have several options in container gardening. You can set up a window box indoors on a windowsill, hang a window box outside your window, or grow plants in pots on your patio or balcony. A good rule is to use small containers in a small space. You can group them to create a larger arrangement, but huge planters tend to overwhelm small spaces. Likewise, don't fill those small containers with large-leaved plants, which will also visually overwhelm the space. What you will be able to grow in those planters, however, depends on several factors. Here are some questions you must answer before you start planting:

- **What will be the purpose of your garden?** Do you intend to grow herbs to cook with or vegetables to eat? Is your garden to be a peaceful retreat, your personal connection to nature, your power place? If you plan well enough, you can create a sacred space where you can carry on your green witch dialogue with nature. Watering, weeding, and caring for a window box can be as rewarding as sitting in the middle of a national park.

- **When will you be using your space?** Will you be gardening or enjoying your space in the daytime or in the evening? Because some plants bloom and release their scent after dark, your plant selection can reflect your schedule.
- **Realistically, how much time will you devote to maintaining your garden?**
- **What is your budget?**
- **Do you want your garden to reflect the style of the rest of your home?** Do you want to do something dramatically different to contrast with your usual style?

Answering these questions and making a list of what you want to get out of gardening will help you determine what kind of garden to develop.

Once you have defined the purpose of your garden, you can begin to focus on how you will go about creating the garden. Make a wish list of all the plants you'd like to work with. The purpose of the garden will help you rule out certain types of plants and focus on others. Find out the ideal climate zone for each of the plants you want to grow. Some of your wish list will inevitably be crossed off because you don't live in the right kind of climate. Read up carefully on the plants that remain on your list. Some will be easy to grow, whereas others will be challenging and energy consuming. Limits to the time and energy you have to devote to your garden will eliminate other plants on your wish list. Next, consider the projected height and diameter of plants you want. You will have to discard some because they will grow too tall or broad for your balcony or patio or containers. Remember, your containers have to be large enough to accommodate the roots of the plants you intend to grow in them.

Light and weather are two other important aspects of working with a small container garden. How much sunlight does your chosen garden space receive per day? What direction does it face? If you face north, stick with shade-loving varieties; if you face east, your garden will receive early-morning sunlight; if you face south, keep a close watch on your garden to ensure that the sun does not burn it or dry out every plant; if you face west, your garden will have the benefit of the warm afternoon sun. If you live on the second story or above, the wind will be harsher, which can play havoc with your plants. Anything extremely delicate will have to be sheltered. If you plant perennials, you will have to protect them during winter or during the fallow part of their cycle.

Artificial light is another consideration. If you intend to spend most of your time in your garden at night, you may wish to add a specialized lighting system to highlight your plants and allow you to see clearly. Hanging lanterns can create a very serene and relaxing atmosphere, but keep safety in mind. If you use candles or oil lamps, keep the wicks low and the flames well protected from the wind. Only use lanterns that have been designed for outdoor use, and keep them away from anything flammable.

Tips on Planting

The urban green witch usually doesn't have a lot of space. While sprouting plants from seed to repot outdoors in a container garden is a wonderful way to forge a connection with your garden from the very first stirrings of life, it is often a challenge. Try it. If nothing sprouts, don't despair. There's no shame in buying hardened seedlings from a nursery or garden center and planting those in your containers.

Be sure to use good potting soil. To ease drainage, blend another medium with it, such as peat moss, and line the base of your container with small stones. Regular garden soil isn't right for container gardens. Container gardens need soil rich in nutrients, because there's so little soil in the container. If garden soil is the only thing available to you, then blend equal parts of sand and peat moss into it. Ask your garden center about fertilizers for container gardens to maintain a high level of nutrients for your plants. Using fertilizer isn't cheating; it's nourishing your plants in an environment that cannot do it on its own.

Regular general maintenance is the key to keeping your garden in balance. Look at your plants every day. Look for yellowed leaves, limp foliage, dead flowers. Nip off dying areas and water dry plants. Clay pots are porous and will lose water faster than glazed or plastic containers. Rotate pots so that all sides of the plant get equal light. Being sensitive to the status of your garden will allow you to pick up on small oddities before they grow into problems.

Your watering schedule will depend on your weather, the size of your containers, and what kind of plants you're growing. Containers tend to not hold a lot of water, because there isn't a lot of earth in them. The water dries up or is rapidly absorbed by the plant. A good rule is to water every couple of days unless you're in a dry spell, in which case water every day. If carrying heavy cans or pitchers of water is difficult for you, consider getting a hose attachment for your kitchen tap.

Caring for Your Garden Naturally

There are several ways to cultivate your garden naturally. After all, the idea of using chemical ingredients on your garden to cultivate growth or kill invading insects is contrary to the green witch way. Here are some tips for using natural methods to increase the bounty of your garden.

COMPOSTING

Composting is the practice of returning organic matter to the earth where it can decompose and add its nutrients to the soil. Although composting is usually thought of as something landowners do, as it traditionally consists of creating a compost pile in the corner of a yard, urban dwellers can also compost easily in a modified fashion. Vermicomposting, or using red worms to break down organic matter, is one option. Vermicomposting kits can be ordered online or obtained from ecological shops or garden centers. A less expensive and easier alternative is a compost bin. You can place the bin outdoors, which most apartment dwellers prefer, but if you have no balcony, you can put it in a dark corner of the kitchen or laundry room.

Compost requires three things: warmth, dark, and food. The warmth is achieved by placing your bin close to the wall if on the balcony or storing it under your sink if indoors. Dark is obtained by using an opaque material for the bin and by having a tight-fitting lid. The food comes from finely chopped vegetable and fruit scraps. Never add meat products or anything with grease to your compost bin. These will decompose, all right, but it will smell dreadful, unbalance the compost you're building, and attract pests. You can add tea leaves (tear open your tea bags if you don't use loose tea) and coffee grounds, eggshells, fruit and vegetable scraps, and dead leaves and flowers pinched off your houseplants and container plants.

The ideal container for composting is a plastic garbage can or a large Tupperware bin. Line the bottom with dead leaves or shredded newspaper. Put a layer of earth on top of that, then add your first batch of chopped food scraps and a bit of water. Stir it with a stick and replace the lid. The lid will hold the humidity inside as the food begins to decompose, but it's a good idea every once in a while to "water" your compost to keep it damp (but not wet). Add a bit more dry material, such as more shredded newspaper or earth, each week to ensure a good balance of carbon and nitrogen. Every time you add more scraps, give the compost a stir to combine the new material with the older compost. Once in a while, give the whole thing a complete turn over with a small shovel or trowel to aerate the soil. In about three months, your compost will be ready for use. Add some to the top of each of your containers and houseplants. Be sure to leave some in your compost bin to start the next batch.

> If you're concerned about smells, don't worry. Good compost has a sweet, rich smell as it decomposes. To keep stronger compost odors at bay, turn it more frequently.

Compost tea is made by filtering water through the compost. This produces a nutrient-rich liquid that you can use to water your houseplants and spray the foliage of your container garden to help nourish and protect the plant both above ground and below. To make a simple compost tea:

1. Loosely fill a bucket a third to halfway full of compost. Give the compost a couple of turns with the trowel to aerate it properly and break up any clumps.
2. Pour warm water (not hot or boiling) over the compost and allow it to sit for two to three days.
3. Carefully decant the resulting brown water into another bucket or pitcher.
4. Allow the wet compost to dry out to its usual damp state before returning it to your compost bin.

You can use the brown compost tea to water your plants or to spray the foliage to battle pests, illness, and pollution damage. Never drink compost tea; it's not for human consumption.

AIR POLLUTION

The green witch living in the city may be exposed to high levels of air pollution. Pollution can create breathing problems, of course, but it also leaves a film of grime everywhere. Not only do your windows become dirty and your walls dull over time, but your garden suffers as well. Leaves can become yellow and limp, growth can be sketchy, and the plant becomes weak. Be loving with your plants. Gently wipe off the dust that accumulates as a result of city life. If you are lucky enough to have a small plot in a city garden, hose it down regularly. Use a spray of compost tea to help nourish the plants and counteract the damage air pollution can cause.

INSECTS AND OTHER PESTS

If you're working with an urban container garden, you'll probably never have to worry about deer or rabbits nibbling your seedlings down to a bare stem poking out of the ground. You will, however, still have to worry about insects.

If your container garden is the haven of the usual numbers of city bugs, then burning citronella candles in the area can somewhat help thin out the insect population. If your plants develop more plant-specific insect infestations, there are a few green witch–friendly things you can do to help. The first thing to remember is that you don't have to resort to chemical insecticides. Using these in a container garden is overkill, and, besides, there are cheaper and kinder alternatives.

Try a natural insecticide. Make an extract of garlic, onion, or hot pepper. Take 3 tablespoons (approximately an ounce and a half) of the vegetable matter and chop it finely or purée it in a blender with a bit of water. Add 2 cups of water to the mixture and allow it to steep overnight or for a full day. Strain it, dilute it so that the total amount of liquid equals 1 liter or 1 quart, and pour it into a spray bottle. Test it on a leaf of the affected plant; if the leaf responds poorly, dilute the spray some more and test again.

In extreme circumstances, you can use a solution of one part bleach to forty parts water to eliminate stubborn pests. Spray this over the foliage and stem of the plant, but do not soak the earth. Rinse well with clear water. This is easier if you place a plastic bag or some such thing over the earth and the container, or tilt the container so that the runoff doesn't land in the pot.

When you spray, no matter what you spray with, remember to practice safe spraying habits:

- Always wear gloves, long sleeves, and a mask when spraying with insecticides, even natural ones. Garlic, onion, and hot pepper can all be very irritating to the mucous membranes. If you inhale the spray, it can cause pain and irritation to the throat and lungs. Don't spray when there is a strong breeze. Wait for a calm day.

- Do not spray during the heat of the day. Do it first thing in the morning or wait until the evening.

- Always perform a test on a small area of each type of plant before you spray them all. This way you can test the strength of the spray as well as the plant's reaction to it.

- Never spray all your plants indiscriminately. These sprays are not all-purpose preventives. They are meant to target a specific problem. They can also kill off the beneficial insects and microbes that live among your plants.

Fill Your Home with Houseplants

If growing plants outdoors is impossible in your situation, or if you want green indoors as well as out, try houseplants.

When you bring home a new houseplant, make sure to do a gentle energy purification to help acclimatize it to the energy of your living space. This also removes any negativity that may be clinging to it. You can do this for outdoor plants as well, though it may not be necessary because planting them in the ground helps stabilize and cleanse the energy clinging to them. You can do a gentle purification simply by running your hand over the plant and holding your palm and fingers about 1 to 2 inches away from the foliage. Visualize scooping up any black or smoky energy you see around the plant. Flick your hand as if you were shaking water off it to remove and disperse the negative energy. If you are concerned about the negative energy affecting the energy of your home, purify new plants before you bring them into your house. If you do the purification inside and feel uncomfortable, burn a purifying incense in the room. Remember, you can never remove the basic energy of an object, so don't worry about removing the positive energy associated with the plant.

To welcome the plant into your home, bless a pitcher of water with a prayer like the following, then use it to water the houseplant:

> *Spirits of Earth, Water, Fire, and Air,*
> *I ask your blessing on this water.*
> *Endow it with strength, protection, and peace,*
> *And may the plants that drink of it be similarly blessed.*

Give your new houseplant as much of this sacred drink as it requires. Use the rest for your current houseplants.

SOME CONSIDERATIONS

Choosing what sorts of houseplants to bring into your home is as important as choosing the plants you grow outdoors. Carefully consider the amount of time and energy you can spare to care for houseplants. Think about the light that fills your living space, the direction from which it comes, and how bright it is. Think about how dry or humid your living space is and the general temperatures. All these things have a great impact upon the plants you can successfully grow where you live. Think, too, about how big your rooms are. Houseplants are limited by their pots, and to grow larger they may need larger containers.

Carefully consider the energy of the plant. How will it fit in and interact with the flow of energy already established in your home? Evaluate the energy by holding your hands over the plant and sensing its energy (see the energy-sensing exercises in Chapter 3). Once you have felt a plant's energy, you will be able to judge whether it will fit into your home's energy or not.

Finally, it is important to remember that like all plants, houseplants absorb negative energy. However, because they are potted in a small amount of earth, they cannot transform the energy with the same success that outdoor plants in the ground can. Be kind to your houseplants. Give them an appropriate fertilizer, repot them before it becomes necessary, and purify them regularly. If you neglect them, they will eventually die from the accumulated negativity. If all your houseplants look sickly, this can be a message that it's time for you to do a complete and thorough house cleansing and purification.

Chapter 7

Create and Craft Green Witch Magic

MAGICAL LORE BASED IN THE GREEN WORLD is the central body of knowledge in the practice of green witchcraft. This chapter examines practical and magical applications, crafts, and spells combining the various elements of the natural world, plus tips on preparation and storage.

When selecting the herbs and other natural elements that you intend to use in your crafts, it is essential to always fully research the herb, magically and medicinally. Carefully read the recommended methods of preparation in your reference books and pay close attention to cautions and notes. Certain herbs, for example, are safe to use externally, but are toxic if taken internally. If you intend to burn the plant matter, verify that the smoke is safe to inhale. In your green witch journal, describe any herb you intend to use, and if there is something to remember, add a note to the label of your preparation. If you are crafting an herbal preparation for someone else, inform yourself of their sensitivities and allergies beforehand and write out a full list of ingredients for their reference.

Preparing Herbs

Check your stock of preserved herbs and plants every year to see what you're low on and what has gone bad. When you harvest plant matter, always make sure that you know what part of the plant to harvest, whether you use leaves, stems, flowers, or the root. Never collect an entire plant. Never pull it up by the roots and take the whole thing home. Take only what you need, and make sure that it's less than a quarter of what's available. In harvesting, less is more. Never assume that you should lay in a huge stock of something. You are unlikely to use it all and you'll end up throwing most of it out. Most green witch projects and charms take only a pinch or spoonful of an herb. It is essential to note in your green witch notebook what plant you are harvesting, where it is being harvested, the date, and how much you are taking.

If you're not using the plant matter fresh, then it must be dried before you store it. Before drying, shake, brush, or wash off any dirt. To air dry it, lay the leaves or flowers out on an old screen or on cheesecloth and allow it to dry in a well-ventilated area. You can also bundle the stems together with an elastic band or string and hang the bunch indoors in a dry place with good air circulation, out of direct sunlight. Tuck a small card with the name of the herb in the bundle to help you identify the plant once it's dry. Don't leave a bundle of herbs hanging for too long, or it will become dusty. To protect it from dust, or if the stem plant has seeds or fragile bits that may fall off as it dries, slip it in a paper bag and secure the bag around the stems with string before hanging it to dry. To prepare a plant for storage, strip the leaves off the stems over a sheet of newspaper or a clean cloth.

You can also dry plant matter in the oven. Chop up the stems roughly, then scatter pieces of stem, plus leaves and flowers, in a single layer on a baking sheet covered with parchment and place it in a barely warm oven (100°F) with the door cracked open for an hour or two, depending on the thickness of the herb you're drying. Check frequently and remove dried matter, leaving the rest to continue drying.

> Opaque containers are best for storing herbs. Ceramic canisters with tight seals and dark glass jars are ideal. Keep an assortment of containers of various sizes on hand. Kitchen shops are a great source for jars, bowls, tins, mortars and pestles, and other useful green witch paraphernalia. You may also want to invest in a cutting board and chopping knives to be used specifically for your green witch work.

If you wish to use the herbs like rosemary or peppermint fresh at a later date, you can pick them and store them in the freezer. For short-term storage, you can simply tumble sturdy leaves into a small paper bag, fold it over, and store it in the freezer door. Be sure to write the herb, the date, and where it was harvested on the bag. To keep herbs longer, rinse them under cold water, blot them dry with a paper towel, chop them roughly, and spread them on a baking sheet. Put the baking sheet in the freezer until the herbs have frozen, then store them in zip-top freezer bags. This method keeps the leaves separate. Mark the bag clearly with the name of the herb, the date, and where you harvested it. To use, simply open the bag and take out what you need. If leaves or flowers have frozen together, take the mass out and chop off what you need with a knife. To freeze individual portions for cooking magic, chop the plant finely and pack a teaspoon or tablespoon of the herb into each compartment of an ice cube tray. Run a bit of water into each compartment over the herb, and freeze. When the herb cubes are frozen, pop them out and place them in zip-top bags. Again, mark the bags with the necessary information.

Remember that when you harvest plant matter an exchange of energy is required. This means that you must give something back in exchange for what you are taking. Bring along a bottle of water and offer the plant a few drops when you harvest some of it. Thank the plant for its kindness in sharing.

Extracting the Energies of Herbs

Herbs and plant matter are most commonly prepared for use in an infusion, which you may better know as tea. Teas aren't used only for consumption, of course, which is why books on magical and spiritual applications use the word "infusion." In this book, if I use the word "tea" I'm referring to something you'll drink; if I use the word "infusion" I'm talking about a liquid that you'll use in some other application.

The basic preparation is known as a "simple," which is a single-herb preparation. This is the best and easiest way to access the energy of an individual plant and the safest way to test new herbs for their effects. The following four methods explain how to extract and preserve the energies and benefits of various herbs:

1. **Infusion** is the process by which leaves and/or flowers are steeped for a period of time in water of a particular temperature. As the water cools, the herbal matter steeps. This is a gentle technique that allows the water to extract the benefits and energies from fragile herbal matter. An infusion creates the weakest extraction.

2. **Decoction** is the process by which denser herbal matter is boiled in water for a specific period of time. This technique is used for roots and twigs and bark. A decoction creates a slightly stronger extraction.

3. **Enfleurage** is the method by which oils and energies are extracted from herbal matter by soaking the herb in an oil or a fat, either heated or at room temperature. The result is an essential oil if the liquid is at room temperature, and a pomade if the result is a solid. Your oil will vary in strength depending on how long you saturate your herbal matter and how frequently you change the depleted herbal matter for fresh. Without professional equipment, it is difficult to make a perfume-grade essential oil with a strong scent at home. While scent is an important aesthetic element, its strength does not necessarily correspond to how much energy is held in the essential oil. A magical oil may not, therefore, have a strong scent. Essential oils are used externally. (To avoid serious illness or accidental poisoning, never use a homemade essential oil internally; only use medicinal-grade essential oils from a reputable company.)

4. **Maceration** is the process by which herbal matter is steeped in a solvent such as vinegar, alcohol, or glycerin. The result is

called a tincture. Tinctures are commonly used for medicinal purposes, usually by adding a few drops to a glass of water or spoonful of honey and consuming it. Tinctures can also be used magically. A tincture will last for many more years than the dried herb. A dried herb loses its flavor and magical potency after one to three years, whereas the tincture preserves the herbal extract.

OTHER HERBAL PREPARATIONS

In both medicine and magic, there are a variety of ways to apply herbal energies. The four methods previously described result in liquids of varying viscosity. To deliver those liquids in methods other than pouring or drinking them, they can be combined with another base to offer a more flexible application. The results of mixing these liquids with another base include the following possibilities:

- **Salves** are created by melting beeswax and adding a liquid extract (usually an oil) to it, then allowing it to cool. Infusions and decoctions are almost useless in preparing a salve because they aren't strong enough to carry the required energy or extract. Salves are rubbed into the body or an object.
- **Liniments** are liquids that are usually alcohol based. A liniment is designed to be rubbed briskly on the body.
- **Soaps** take your liquid extracts and combine them with a base of fats designed to raise dirt from a surface, enabling it to be washed away. Magical soaps are particularly interesting because they also pull negative or undesirable energy from an object and allow it to be washed away. A magical soap removes undesirable energies and leaves desired energies.

Blessing Your Creations

Although everything has an innate energy and you empower every preparation or craft object you create with your intention, sometimes it's nice to seal or enhance the combined energies. Performing an elemental blessing upon an object can help dedicate it to the purpose you intend it for. It also sends a signal to your own psyche that your work is finished and is now performing the function for which it was designed.

ELEMENTAL BLESSING

This blessing can be performed as the final step of any project or upon new objects or items intended for a shrine. In essence, this act purifies the object and then blesses it with positive energy.

The following blessing is written with the assumption that the object you will bless is small enough to be held in your hands. If it is not, place it on or next to your workspace and adjust your actions accordingly.

If you have previously cleansed the object you intend to bless, or if you have empowered it, you may skip steps 2 through 6.

- Small dish of salt or earth (or a small crystal or other stone)
- Stick of incense in a holder, or herbal incense and a self-lighting charcoal briquette in a heatproof dish
- Candle in candleholder
- Small dish of water
- Matches or a lighter
- Object to be blessed

1. Arrange each elemental symbol on your workspace, either in a square or in a line. Light the incense and the candle. Take three deep breaths to release stress so you can focus on your task.

2. Pick up the object with one hand or lay it on your workspace in front of you. With your other hand, take a pinch of the salt or earth and sprinkle it gently over the object (or take the crystal or stone in your hand and touch it to the object), saying:

    By earth I cleanse you.

3. Pick up the candle and pass it around the object in a counterclockwise direction, saying:

    By fire I cleanse you.

4. Pick up the incense and pass it counterclockwise around the object, saying:

    By air I cleanse you.

5. Touch your fingertips to the water and sprinkle it over the object, saying:

    By water I cleanse you.

6. Close your eyes, take three slow breaths, and focus on the object.

7. Take another pinch of earth or salt and sprinkle it over the object (or touch the crystal or stone to it), saying:

    You are blessed by earth.

8. Pass the object carefully over the candle flame, making sure not to burn yourself or the object, saying:

    You are blessed by fire.

9. Pass the object through the smoke of the incense, saying:

    You are blessed by air.

10. Touch your fingertips to the water and sprinkle it on the object, saying:

    You are blessed by water.

11. Hold the object up in the air, or if it is too heavy place your hands upon it where it lies, and say:

I ask the Green Spirit of the Universe to bless this object in the name of Earth and of all Nature.

Making Herbal Incense

If you use incense in stick form, then you are familiar with the sweet and gentle smoke created by lighting one end of the stick, gently blowing out the flame, and resting the stick in a censer or incense boat to smolder slowly.

Herbal incense is a completely different experience. It is a wonderful method of experimenting with the bounty of nature. When you create your own herbal incense, you can mix and match the kinds of magical energies you wish to weave together, tailoring them precisely to your specific goal. You can make as much or as little as you like, empowering the blend with your own personal energy.

Herbal incense must always be made with dried herbs. Fresh herbs will not burn correctly and will rot if you attempt to store them. If the only sample of the herb you wish to use in your blend is fresh, then spread the herb on a baking sheet and place it in a barely warm oven (100°F) for forty-five minutes to an hour, watching it carefully. Alternatively, you can spread the herb in a single layer on a paper towel and microwave it for thirty seconds on high. Check to see how dry it is. You can microwave in ten-second increments for further drying. Some green witches, concerned that the microwave damages the herb's energy, recoil in horror at the idea of microwaving their herbs, whereas other green witches have no qualms about using modern equipment such as a microwave, a juicer, or an electric coffee grinder to prepare their magical supplies. It's your choice. As a modern green witch, use what you have at your disposal, as long as you feel comfortable with it.

TEST YOUR HERBS

Before you blend herbal incense, it's important to do some research to find out what kinds of herbs and flowers are best for your recipe. Before you mix and burn any herb or combination of herbs, it is important to look up the toxicity of each plant. If it's poisonous to touch or eat, chances are the smoke is also poisonous to breathe. Don't take chances.

Once you have a short list of the herbs you'd like to use in your magical incense, take an hour or so to light a single charcoal briquette and drop a tiny pinch of each herb by itself onto the ignited surface. Burning herbal matter will not smell like the fresh herb. In fact, it usually smells like some sort of variation on burning leaves or grass clippings. Testing each herb alone will give you an idea of what it smells like. As it burns, make notes in your green witch journal about the smell, the density of the smoke, how quickly the herb is consumed, and what kind of energy you sense it giving off as it smolders. Also make a note of how you react physically to the herb. It is better to discover now in a test run that you react badly to a certain herb than when you're attempting to use it magically.

Once you've tested each herb, you're ready to work with proportions. Do you want to add more of one herb and perhaps only a pinch of another? Much of the green witch's work is intuitive, which means that you'll feel drawn to something without necessarily having solid information or reasoning to support your feeling.

RESINS

One of the plain truths about using herbal incense is that it doesn't always smell as sweet as store-bought stick incense. Adding resin in an equal amount to your herbal blend will not only improve the incense's burn rate, but will also provide a more agreeable base note to your burning incense. Resins have been used for centuries in various cultures as sweet-smelling offerings to the gods. They carry various magical associations just as herbs do.

Before adding one or more resins to an herbal blend, however, drop a single grain of the resin or a tiny pinch of powder onto a charcoal briquette to acquaint yourself with the scent of the resin on its own. Make notes in your journal as to the scent of the resin as it melts on the charcoal, the density of smoke it produces, the energy it gives off, and how it makes you feel. (See instructions on how to use charcoal briquettes later on in this chapter.)

While the release of certain energies is the primary goal of green witch magic, aesthetics are also important. To that end, I advise using one or more of the following resins as a base for your herbal incense (remember that the amount of resin should equal the total amount of herbal matter).

COPAL

This resin comes in various shades of white, gold, and black, and the scent is slightly different for each kind. Golden copal is most common, and if you pick up a packet marked simply "copal," that's what it's likely to be. Copal is the petrified sap of the *Bursera odorata* and has an appealing sweet scent that makes an excellent base for floral or lighter herbal incense blends. Copal carries an energy that is particularly good for love, house blessings, dedications, meditation, protection, celebration, solar energy, and creating sacred space.

FRANKINCENSE

One of the most popular resins, the golden-toned frankincense is the solidified sap of the *Boswellia carterii* tree, sometimes called the olibanum. It has a slightly spicy-sweet scent and makes an excellent all-purpose base for just about any herbal incense. Frankincense is traditionally associated with sanctity, purification, meditation, protection, joy, celebration, solar energy, and consecration.

MYRRH

Another common resin, myrrh is brownish and has a darker, slightly bittersweet scent. It comes from the *Commiphora myrrha*, or gum myrrh tree, and carries the magical associations of sanctity, honoring the dead and the spirit world, purification, and healing. Myrrh adds a bit of extra power to any herbal incense; adding just a grain or two will do the job.

BENZOIN

This grayish resin is usually found in powdered form. It comes from the *Styrax benzoin* tree and has a light, clean, slightly sweet scent. It is excellent for purifying, healing, prosperity, and attraction in general.

STYRAX

Sometimes spelled storax, this black resin is a softer, earthier resin than those previously listed. It comes from the *Liquidambar styraciflua* tree. It is excellent for healing and grounding.

DRAGON'S BLOOD

This red resin is the petrified sap of the palm tree known as *Daemonorops draco*, or the dragon's blood palm. It is one of the key ingredients in violin stain. It is remarkably sticky and will cling to your fingers and tools. Dragon's blood is frequently used for protection, purification, and as a general addition to your spells as an all-purpose power boost.

SANDALWOOD

Often blended into herbal incenses or used as a base, sandalwood isn't technically a resin, but a powdered or shredded wood. Available both in red (*Adenanthera pavonina*) and white (*Santalum album*), sandalwood is generally associated with spirituality, purification, meditation, peace, healing, and protection.

Resins are usually sold by weight in packets of rough grains or chips. Generally, it is best to powder your resin before blending it with your herbal matter. This will entail a bit of grinding on your part with a stone mortar and pestle (wood is unsuitable for grinding resins) or using a small coffee grinder reserved only for grinding herbs and resins. The powdered resin will blend better with the dried herbs and yield a smoother burn.

BLENDING HERBAL INCENSE

When you create a recipe for herbal incense, look at the purpose for which you are creating it and select a combination of herbs and resins that will support that goal with their energies. For example, a prosperity incense may include one part benzoin as the resin base, with one part herbal blend of mint, basil, and cinnamon, all of which are associated with prosperity. Like other witches, green witches often like to work in multiples of three on top of their base ingredient. Three is a number associated with the Goddess. You may also like to work with a multiple of four to honor the four elements. There's no firm rule, however, as to how many or how few resins or herbs to use in an incense; use what you feel drawn to using. But remember that more is not necessarily better.

The basic steps to blending herbal incense are simple. If necessary, gently grind the resin until the pieces are in small granules. Be careful not to overgrind them, or the heat produced by the mortar and pestle or coffee grinder will make the resin sticky. Crumble or powder the dried herbs and place them in the jar with the resin. Cap it and shake until the ingredients are well blended. Don't forget to write the final recipe in your journal, along with the magical purpose and the date on which you blended it, and label the container.

To further enhance your herbal incense, you may add up to three drops of essential oil to the mixture before you cap and shake it. Again, consider your magical goal and choose an appropriate essential oil. You may use the oil of an herb or resin that is already a part of your blend to strengthen that particular scent or another oil to add a different energy to the blend. Do not use more than three drops, or the incense will be too wet to burn.

Once your herbal incense is blended, you may use it right away or leave it to sit and allow the energies to blend for a week or so before using it.

EMPOWERING HERBAL INCENSE

You can use the incense as it is. However, like any other magical craft or preparation, empowering the incense will weave the energies together better and focus them specifically upon your magical goal.

There are two ways to empower your herbal incense. Most green witches employ them both. The first is to visualize your magical goal as you grind and blend each herb and resin. This method allows you to program each component separately. The second method is as follows:

1. Hold the jar of finished incense in your hands. Take three deep breaths to focus. Think of your magical goal.

2. Visualize a sparkling light forming around the jar in your hands. This sparkling light is the energy that empowers the incense, the energy associated with your magical goal.

3. Imagine the sparkling light being absorbed into the blend of resins and herbs. The herbal incense has now been energized with your magical goal. It is empowered for that use.

BURNING HERBAL INCENSE

Herbal incense is burned on small, round charcoal briquettes that are available at New Age and religious supply shops. To burn herbal incense, you will require the following three things:

1. A small, round briquette of self-igniting charcoal (this is NOT barbecue charcoal)
2. A heatproof censer with a layer of sand or earth in it
3. A lighter or long-stemmed matches

Self-igniting charcoal briquettes come in various sizes. I don't recommend the ½-inch size, as they are easy to smother with a spoonful of incense and prone to falling apart or exploding if not handled correctly. I recommend buying the 1-inch briquettes and using half a briquette at a time (you really don't need a whole briquette for a single spoonful of herbal incense). A briquette will burn for forty-five minutes to an hour, and burning a spoonful of herbal incense doesn't take long at all.

Caution: Never, ever use outdoor barbecue charcoal, as it releases dangerous fumes that can be fatal when used indoors or in a poorly ventilated space.

A single spoonful of incense is usually all you'll need to release its energy into your space. A scant teaspoonful sprinkled on a glowing charcoal will release a cloud of smoke. Unlike stick incense, herbal incense burns all at once until it is gone, and thus releases more smoke and scent over a shorter period of time. The energy and scent linger in the space, however, so there's no need to keep piling on the incense blend to produce a steady supply of smoke. If you try to burn too much incense, the room will become too smoky and it's likely to set off your smoke detector. With herbal incense, a little goes a long way. When you use herbal incense, you're actually smoldering it, not burning it—there's no flame involved. The bits of resin melt and the herbal matter turns black and crackles away.

If you choose to use matches to light the charcoal, long-stemmed matches are preferable because short safety matches burn down too quickly. A long-handled barbecue lighter is ideal for lighting charcoal briquettes. Although there are a few brave souls who hold the charcoal with fingers while they light it, I don't recommend this for obvious safety reasons. The best way to light charcoal is to hold it in one hand with a pair of tweezers or a small pair of tongs while you apply the flame to the charcoal with your other hand. Hold the flame to the edge of the briquette, and as it catches fire it will begin to sparkle. If your charcoal is particularly quick, those sparkles will begin to move across the surface of the briquette, firing the rest of the surface. If your charcoal is very densely made or slightly damp because of humidity in the environment, you may have to hold the flame to different areas to light as many as possible before they combine to ignite the rest of the briquette. Remember that your tweezers or tongs are metal and will conduct the heat of the charcoal briquette once it begins to ignite.

When the briquette has fully ignited, lay it down carefully on the layer of sand or earth in your censer. You can use almost any heatproof dish as a censer, as long as it has a layer of material to absorb the heat of the charcoal. To be on the safe side, you can put a trivet or heatproof coaster under your censer to protect your table or altar from heat damage.

Wait until the sparkles have finished coursing across the surface of the briquette and the surface has begun to glow faintly red. At this point, your charcoal is ready to receive a teaspoonful of herbal incense or a pinch of resin. Some people prefer to wait until there is a thin layer of gray ash on top of the briquette before sprinkling incense on it.

Don't just pile a heaping spoonful of the herbal incense on the charcoal briquette. Sprinkle it gently, visualizing the goal for which you've created the blend. A solid chunk of incense can smother the charcoal briquette.

When the incense has finished burning, you can wait fifteen or twenty minutes for the smoke to dissipate a bit, then sprinkle another half-teaspoon of incense on the charcoal. When this has burned away, leave the charcoal to burn out on its own. It will turn to gray ash. Allow this ash to cool, then stir it gently into the sand or earth in your censer.

Keeping a small bottle of water or a second bowl of earth or sand nearby to smother the charcoal and incense should it somehow get out of control is always an intelligent precaution.

STORING HERBAL INCENSE

When you make your first trial batch of herbal incense, make it in a small quantity so that if you don't like it you won't be stuck with a whole bottle of the stuff. Mark down the proportions of the recipe so that if you like it, you can increase it easily.

I keep my herbal incense in small spice jars in a dark cupboard. I also use 4-ounce (125-ml) canning jars. Baby food jars are also ideal, so if you have a child or know someone who does, ask for empty jars, wash them well, and make sure they're completely dry before you use them. Always make sure to clearly label the jar. Write the name of the incense and the date on the cap with a grease pencil or on a self-stick label. No matter how firmly you believe that you'll remember exactly what the blend is for by the scent or the look of the incense, I guarantee that you won't. The date is important because you will be able to look at your green witch journal and see what else was going on when you blended that incense (and perhaps exactly what inspired the blend in the first place). Three to five years from now, you'll know that you have to make up a fresh batch for magical use and throw the old one out (or use the old one for perfume properties only).

Suggested recipes for the seven central energies of the green witch:

- Happiness: frankincense, lemon, orange
- Harmony: lavender, white sandalwood powder, jasmine
- Health: myrrh, benzoin, hyssop, eucalyptus
- Love: copal, rose, jasmine, cinnamon
- Peace: frankincense, lavender, violet
- Prosperity: frankincense, pine, basil, mint, cinnamon
- Protection: dragon's blood, rosemary, clove

Create Spell Bags

Spell bags, which are small fabric bags into which you place a variety of objects and items chosen for their magical associations, are used in various magical applications. Spell bags can be made in any size and used anywhere. You can hang one above the door, tuck one into your car's glove compartment, tuck them in drawers, handbags, hang them on bedposts...the only limit is your imagination.

Here is a basic small protection-charm project. Use it as a basis for creating your own spell bags.

PROTECTION CHARM

This spell bag is designed to be hung above your front or back door, whichever is used more frequently.

- 2 (3 × 5-inch) pieces of red or black fabric
- Iron (optional)
- Thread to match
- Needle
- Pins
- 1 (12-inch) length of red yarn or narrow ribbon

- 1 snowflake obsidian
- 1 teaspoon caraway seeds
- 1 teaspoon mugwort
- Pinch of salt

1. Make a small hem along one of the short sides of the fabric rectangle as follows: Fold the edge of one of the 3-inch-long sides of one cloth rectangle down ¼ inch, wrong side to wrong side, and press into place with your fingers or the iron. Using a running stitch, sew the edge down. Repeat on the other piece of cloth.

2. Place the cloth rectangles face to face, right side to right side, matching edges. (The folded edge will be facing out on both.) Pin into place.

3. Using a running stitch, sew along the three raw edges of the rectangle. Leave the side with the hems open. Turn the pouch right side out.

4. Fold the yarn or ribbon in half. Secure the fold to the outside of one of the side seams of the pouch with a couple of small stitches.

5. Into this small pouch, place the snowflake obsidian and the herbs.

6. Tie the spell bag shut with the yarn or ribbon. Hang from a small nail above your door.

By using a tie on the spell bag, you can open it and add other items as needed to supplement the magical energy. Spell bags can also be sewn shut, like small pillows, although if this is done they should not be opened.

If there comes a time when the spell bag is no longer required, or if the usefulness is past, then undo or unpick the spell bag and separate the items inside. Dispose of them separately, adding the herbs to your garden or compost.

Craft a Dream Pillow

Another form of spell bag, the dream pillow allows the gentle energies of the herbs to interact with your own energy while you sleep. Tuck the dream pillow under your bed pillow, hang it on your bedpost, or set it on your bedside table. Made on a larger scale, dream pillows can become herbal pillows.

When making dream or herb pillows, the amount of magic you apply is up to you. An ideal way to reinforce the magical goal of the herbs in the dream pillow is to choose cloth of an appropriate color you associate with the magical goal. If you add a ribbon to the pillow for hanging, choose an appropriate length to slip over the bedpost or hang on a nail in the wall by your bed.

SWEET DREAMS PILLOW

This pillow is designed to encourage relaxation and soothe restless sleep.

- 1 tablespoon violets
- 1 tablespoon spearmint
- 2 tablespoons lavender
- Small bowl
- 1 (8 × 4–inch) rectangle of cloth (your choice of color)
- Thread to match
- Pins
- Needle
- Iron (optional)
- Cotton batting (about the size of your fist, or 2 (4 × 4–inch) squares)
- Ribbon (optional; for length, see previous paragraph)

1. Blend the herbs in the bowl with your fingertips.

2. Fold the rectangle of cloth over onto itself so that you have a square of doubled material. If you are using a fabric with a design, make sure the design is on the inside. Pin the two halves together.

3. Using a running stitch, sew along two of the three open sides of the fabric square, leaving one side open.

4. Fold approximately ¼ inch of the raw edge of the open side down on what is currently the outside of the pouch. Finger–press the edge so that it stays creased, or use the iron. Turn the fabric pouch right side out, so that the seams are to the inside. (The raw edge of the pressed side should be inside the pouch.)

5. Tease out your cotton or cotton batting so it is fluffier and larger. Place the herbs in the center of the cotton and fold the edges inward so that the herbs are rolled inside the cotton. If the cotton batting is flat, lay one of the squares down, pour the herbs in the middle, lay the second square on top, and secure all four sides with a running stitch.

6. Tuck the herbs in the cotton batting inside the fabric pouch. Pin the open side closed. If you are adding a ribbon hanger, fold your piece of ribbon and insert the ends into the open side of the pouch and pin them into place. Sew the pillow closed with a running stitch, sewing the ribbon into place as you go.

7. Tuck your new dream pillow under your bed pillow or place next to your pillow before you sleep.

You can increase the size of this pillow. The larger you make it, however, the more cotton batting you will need to protect the herbs inside. You may use as many or as few herbs as you like. Here are some suggested blends for dream pillows:

- Peace: lavender, poppy, gardenia
- Harmony: chamomile, violet, calendula
- Happiness: honeysuckle, sunflower
- Love: rose, jasmine, gardenia
- Health: eucalyptus, nutmeg, carnation
- Prosperity: cinnamon, orange, basil
- Protection: geranium, sage, clove

Garden Spell Bags

This type of bag is separate from the general spell bags because it calls for a slightly different approach. Because a garden spell bag is designed to decompose and fall apart, it requires a different set of ingredients and supplies.

A garden spell bag is a charm designed to be hung outside or buried in a particular place. These bags are generally made for protection of the property, protection for a particular area on the property such as a special plant or bed, or to increase the fertility of the garden in general. Because these bags are hung outdoors in the elements, they're generally small; this is for convenience as well as aesthetics. As the bag decomposes, the herbs you stuffed in it start falling out of it. Herbs falling out of a large bag would become untidy. A smaller spell bag ensures less of a mess, as well as a lower-profile charm. If you want to make a larger protective charm of some kind, think about a stepping stone (see later in this chapter) or something made of a more permanent material.

Another reason to keep this garden charm smaller than a regular spell bag or dream pillow is that you will be filling it completely with herbs, not using batting or stuffing. To make the charm, cut out two squares or rectangles and sew them together, as directed in the dream pillow section. Eliminate the stuffing or batting, and simply fill the bag with herbs. Sew the last side shut, adding a hanger as directed in the dream pillow project or a ribbon tie as in the spell bag, and hang it in an appropriate place outdoors.

When you design a garden spell bag, be sure to select a material woven of natural fibers, preferably 100 percent cotton, although wool and silk are acceptable. Natural fiber will ensure that the material decomposes completely and without damage to the environment. You can choose the color according to your magical intention or use a neutral color, like white or unbleached cotton. Remember, however, that the rain will soak the pillow and the herbs inside will stain the fabric; the sun will also bleach it, affecting the color almost immediately. Do not, therefore, expect your garden charm to look beautiful for more than a few days. The processes of bleaching or staining and decomposition are part of the magic: the gradual destruction of the physical charm releases the energy. When the fabric has worn through, you can choose to bury the bag in a selected spot or in your compost heap. Replacing garden charms can become part of your regular magical maintenance of your garden space. You can either make the same spell bag (and write down the new date in your green witch journal so that you keep track of how often you have to replace the charm) or you can evaluate your garden's current needs and design a new one (again, noting the date and new supplies you use and why).

If you add a stone to your garden spell bag, you may choose to bury it with the rest of the remains or to reuse it in your next charm. Reusing the stone is a nice way to maintain continuity with the energy of your garden, even if the herbs you use are different. Do not include metal charms or add nonbiodegradable substances to the herbal mixture, as they can poison the garden.

Make a Broom

In Chapter 2 you learned how to use a broom to purify an area. Finding a natural-bristle broom can be a challenge. But there's no need to despair. Making her own tools is a time-honored practice for a witch of any kind, and making a broom is particularly easy.

CREATE A TWIG BROOM

Gather twigs and a longer stick from below the trees where you live so your broom is a tool tied in to the energy of your particular geographic location. Mixed with your own personal energy, this natural energy will create a broom vibrating with green witch power! Try to identify the trees from which you gather your twigs. The more you know about your supplies, the more tuned in to their energy you'll be.

If you have trees on your own land, save twigs and a long stick during your annual pruning. Otherwise, you can usually walk residential streets in the fall and gather twigs from the piles of pruned material lying on the curbside for rubbish pickup. Ask the resident's permission to take the branches and twigs if they're lying on private property. If the wood you pick up is wet, allow it to dry in a protected, ventilated space, such as a garage or your basement, for a couple of weeks.

When making a broom, it is important to wind the leather tightly around the twigs. The tension is part of what keeps the twigs on the end of the broom.

- Work gloves (optional)
- Newspaper
- 1 stout stick, approximately 5 feet long, between ¾ and 1 inch in diameter
- Saw (optional)
- Sandpaper
- Twigs approximately 18 inches long, no thicker than ¼ inch each (enough to make a 3-inch pile when you gather them together in your hands)
- Wood glue
- Leather strip or cord, 5 feet long, at least ¾ inch wide
- 4 finishing nails
- Hammer

1. Cover your work area with newspaper.
2. Take the 5-foot stick and decide which end will be the top of the handle and which end will be the sweeping end. If the stick has bark on it, decide whether you wish to strip it off or keep it on. If you're using a branch broken off a tree, you may wish to saw the top end flat. Sand the top end of the handle so that no sharp edges or splinters remain.
3. Sort through the pile of smaller sticks and cut or break off any that have other twigs sticking out at odd angles. With the saw, trim them all to roughly 18 inches long.
4. Take one of the thicker twigs and set it against the bottom end of the broom's handle. Overlap the ends of the twig and the broom handle so that approximately 5–6 inches of the twig is lying against the bottom

5 inches of the broom. (The twig will extend about a foot past the end of the broom.) Dot wood glue along those overlapping 5 inches and press the twig against the broom. Laying one end of the leather strip across the twig, add a drop of wood glue to secure it to the wood. Holding it together firmly, hammer one of the finishing nails through the leather strip and the twig into the broom.

5. Spread a thin layer of glue around the bottom 5 inches of the broom and begin to add additional 18-inch twigs, overlapping the top 5–6 inches of each twig against the bottom 5 inches of the broom. Place the second twig over the leather strip, then the next twig under it. Make sure you maintain a consistent tension on the leather strip.

6. When you reach the first twig again, dot some more glue along the top 5 inches of the first layer of twigs and continue adding more twigs, still alternating the leather strip above and below twigs. Remember to keep the twigs wrapped tight. Don't worry about making sure the ends of the twigs are perfectly even. This is a handmade broom and a tool of magic designed to sweep air and energy, not an even floor. It doesn't have to be perfect.

7. When you have reached the halfway point of the second layer, opposite where you started, hold the leather taut and hammer a second finishing nail through it and the twig into the first layer of twigs and the handle below. Continue adding twigs.

8. Continue adding the twigs to the broom, dotting more wood glue along the tops of the twigs as you begin another layer. Keep winding the leather over and under the twigs.

9. When you are satisfied with the thickness of the twig end of the broom, or when you come to the end of your pile of twigs, hammer another nail into the leather and the twigs through to the broom

handle. Dot more glue along the inside of the rest of the leather strip and wrap the leather around and around the twigs. Pull it tight. Secure the end of the leather with a final dot of glue and one final nail.

10. Allow the broom to rest flat (not dangling) on a table or floor for at least thirty-six hours, or until the glue has completely dried. If you wish to further decorate your broom by winding leather around the handle, adding feathers or shells or stones, or by carving it, do so when the glue is dry.

11. Before you use your new magical broom for the first time, empower it by holding it in your hands and visualizing a sparkling white light glowing around it. See the sparkling energy being absorbed into the broom. If you like, you may further bless it with the four elements (see the Elemental Blessing in this chapter).

Craft Balms or Perfumes

This magical craft takes an essential oil of your choice and makes it a solid balm, which can be used as a magical perfume. The term "balm" indicates comfort of some kind, as well as a solid substance that melts when applied to the warmth of the skin.

It is important to remember that balms are magical in nature, which means that the energies of the oils act upon the energy of the individual who uses them.

Make sure the jar, tin, or container you choose to contain the balm has a wide enough mouth for you to reach inside with your fingers. Choose a container that isn't too deep and make sure that the lid closes tightly to preserve the contents as long as possible.

Also be sure to carefully research the oils you wish to use. You don't want to use too much of an oil, like cinnamon, that can irritate your skin. Always consider your skin's sensitivity.

When applying the balm, use only a small amount. Scoop up a bit on your fingertip and rub it gently with a circular motion on the area where you wish to apply it. Do not allow the balm to come in contact with your eyes. Wash your hands after you have used the balm or after the ritual activity you wish to be enhanced by the balm. In the summer, keep your balm in the fridge for a cooling sensation when you apply it.

Balms should not be applied to the skin of children.

MAGICAL BALM

Remember to label the tin or container clearly with the name of the balm. Write the recipe in your green witch journal.

- 1½ teaspoons beeswax beads
- ¼ cup sweet almond oil or jojoba oil
- Small, clean, empty can
- Saucepan and water
- 5–9 drops essential oil(s) of your choice
- 1 teaspoon vitamin E oil (optional)
- Small jar or container

1. Place the beeswax beads and the almond or jojoba oil in the small, clean can. Do NOT cover the can. Place the can in a saucepan filled approximately half-full with water. (This creates a double boiler and keeps the flammable oils from coming into contact with flame or heating coils.) Set the saucepan on the stove over medium heat and allow the heat of the water to melt the beeswax and almond or jojoba oil.

2. Remove the saucepan from the stove. Wearing oven mitts to protect your hands, remove the can from the water bath. Swirl in the drops of essential oil and the vitamin E oil. As you do this, empower the mixture with your magical intent.

3. Allow the mixture to cool slightly. As it cools, the surface will solidify. Using a chopstick or a Popsicle stick, stir it gently to recombine the solid with the liquid. As you stir, reinforce your magical intent.

4. When the mixture has cooled but before it is completely solid, pour it into the clean jar or container and seal it. Label it with the contents and the date.

5. To use the balm, scoop a small amount onto a fingertip and smooth onto your skin.

Here are some suggestions for balms:

- For a **meditation balm**, use 3 drops of lavender, 3 drops of sandalwood, and 2 drops of violet. Rub a small amount into your temples and the inside of your wrists. This is also an excellent blend to use for relaxation and to aid sleep, and it thus doubles as a peace and harmony balm.

- For a **purification balm**, use 2 drops of lavender oil, 3 drops of frankincense, and 3 drops of jasmine. Dot a small amount on your third eye (in the center of your forehead), on your chest, and on the solar plexus. Use whenever you wish to clear negative emotion or energy from your emotional or physical body.

- For a **love balm**, use 3 drops of rose oil, 3 drops of jasmine, 2 drops of lavender oil, and 1 drop of vanilla oil. Dot on the inside of your wrists, over your heart, at the nape of your neck, and behind your knees. (Note that this balm is a general love blend.

It can be used for self-love and affection as well as any other sort of purpose associated with love.)

- For an **abundance balm**, use 1 drop of cinnamon, 2 drops of orange, 3 drops of mint, and 2 drops of pine. Rub a small amount in the palms of your hands and on the soles of your feet.
- For a **healing balm**, use 2 drops of rosemary, 2 drops of eucalyptus, 2 drops of myrrh, and 2 drops of sandalwood. This balm can be used for spiritual, emotional, and physical healing. This is particularly good used on the chest or back. Avoid using this balm near eyes or mucous membranes, or on thin or sensitive skin, because rosemary and eucalyptus can irritate.
- For a **happiness balm**, use 1 drop of lime oil, 2 drops of lemon oil, 2 drops of rose oil, and 2 drops of lavender oil. Apply to the wrists or the back of the hands, the knees, the feet, and over your heart. For a bright, citrus-based happiness balm, use 2 drops of lime oil, 2 drops of lemon oil, 2 drops of orange oil, and 2 drops of bergamot oil.

Build Garden Stepping Stones

This magical craft incorporates herbs, gems or crystals, and any other natural element you wish to include.

Following are two different kinds of stepping stones. The first calls for you to mix and pour your own concrete; the second uses a premade concrete or stone slab purchased from a garden center. Each method produces a different magical stepping stone, but with imagination you can substitute one set of magical supplies for the other, or come up with your own combinations for your own goals.

Once your stepping stone is decorated and varnished, keep it inside for another week to ensure that it has completely cured. During the pouring process and while the stone is drying, do not move the mold.

When you place your stepping stone outside, consider carefully the area best suited for it. While these are commonly called "stepping stones," they are often very unsuitable for being actually walked on because of the raised decorations set into them and the detail you may put into embellishing them. Placing them in a garden near a patio or walkway where they can be seen but not disturbed is often the best choice.

Although these stepping stones are theoretically weatherproof, to avoid crumbling or breakage you may wish to bring them inside for storage if you live in a climate with a severe winter. Inspect your stepping stone every couple of weeks or so to see how it's holding up to the elements. If you use too much water in your concrete mix, the stepping stone may slowly crumble away. If that happens, make a note in your green witch journal to use less water next time, and declare this stepping stone to be a time-release spell. When it has degraded beyond recognition, or to a point where you no longer wish to display it, then remove it with respect, thank it for its work, and dispose of it in the trash. Do not bury it, as not all the supplies you may use will be biodegradable.

PROTECTIVE STEPPING STONE

Place this stone in your garden or by your front door to extend its protective energy to the area. This magical craft is best done outside, and it's best to wear an apron over your work clothes. While it will only take approximately two hours to make the basic stone, it will take at least three days for it to dry.

- Newspaper
- Rubber gloves
- 1 (1-foot × 1-foot) piece of screening
- Aluminum foil pie plate (at least 2 inches deep)
- 1 tablespoon each of three protective herbs (your choice; try angelica, rosemary, and cloves)
- Paint stirrer
- Small bag of concrete mix (quick-setting, or a special stepping-stone blend)
- Bucket
- Water
- Measuring cup
- Old serving spoon (optional)
- 4 obsidian stones in the shape of arrowheads
- Twig or Popsicle stick (optional)
- Acrylic paints and brushes (optional)
- Clear varnish (a spray varnish is easiest) (optional)

1. Spread the newspaper over your work surface to protect it.
2. Put on the rubber gloves and cut the screening to fit inside your pie plate. The screening will serve to reinforce your stepping stone once the stone is dry.
3. Blend the herbs together and set them aside.
4. Use the paint stirrer to mix the concrete powder with the water in the bucket. A proportion of five parts concrete to one part water generally works well, but read the directions on your bag. Add more powder to thicken it, more water to thin it. The mixture should be thick and wet, but not splashy—more like drop-cookie dough than cake batter. Do

not make up the entire bag. Use only as much as you think you'll need to fill the pie plate (with a bit extra just to make sure).

5. Pour or spoon the concrete into the aluminum pie plate (the mold), filling it approximately half-full. Tap the mold to release any air bubbles, and use the stirrer to smooth the concrete out.

6. Lay the screening on top of the concrete in the mold. Pour more concrete on top of the screening, filling the mold approximately ⅔ full. Tap the mold again to release any air bubbles.

7. Sprinkle the herbs on top of the concrete, visualizing their protective energy spreading through the concrete.

8. Pour more concrete on top of the herbs, filling the mold completely. Tap the mold a third magical time to release any air bubbles.

9. Leave the mold to rest for approximately thirty minutes to one hour (check the instructions on your bag of concrete mix). This will allow it to set slightly and give you a firmer surface into which to press the stones.

10. Place the four obsidian stones in a starburst shape in the middle of the stone, with the flat ends forming a square in the center and the points facing the edge of the circle. Firmly press them into the surface of the concrete. As you do, visualize the arrows repelling any negativity that approaches the stone.

11. If you desire, use a twig or a Popsicle stick to draw symbols or write words on the surface of the stone.

12. Now set the stepping stone aside in a safe place to cure for at least two days, preferably three. Again, verify the instructions on your bag of concrete. You may want to leave it longer to be on the safe side so your stone won't crumble if you take it out of the mold before it has completely dried.

13. Pop the stone out of the mold by turning it over and placing it on the newspaper-protected surface. Gently loosen the sides and peel the aluminum pie plate away from the stone. Turn the stone over so that the obsidian starburst is on top.

14. If you choose, you may paint the stone. Once the paints have dried, coat all sides of the stone with a clear varnish to protect the surface.

HAPPINESS STEPPING STONE

This stone attracts joy and laughter. Place it by your front door to invite this energy into your home. With this project, it is best to use a small precast stone as a base because you'll be covering the entire surface with your chosen gems and crystals. This technique uses mortar and grout to affix the decorations to the precast stone.

- Blank paper larger than the precast stepping stone
- Pencil
- Plain precast concrete garden stepping stone
- A selection of tumbled gems and stones such as citrine, tiger's eye, moonstone, sodalite, or rose quartz
- Heavy rubber gloves
- Bucket or clean plastic ice-cream container
- Thin-set mortar
- Paint stirrer
- Water
- Mortar trowel
- Tile grout
- Old rubber spatula
- Sponge
- Soft cloth

1. Trace the stepping stone on the blank paper, then set the stepping stone aside. On the paper, arrange the gems and stones in a pleasing pattern inside the outline of the stepping stone. Use enough stones to fill the outline almost completely, but the gems should not quite touch each other. Set the paper and stones carefully aside.

2. Rinse the blank stepping stone in water to remove any dirt. Washing it under the garden hose will work well.

3. Put on the rubber gloves. In the bucket, mix the thin-set mortar according to the package directions. Do not mix up the entire package. Blend only as much as you think you'll need for this project, with a little bit left over just to be sure. You'll need to cover the surface of your precast stone to a depth of approximately ½ inch.

4. Using the trowel, spread a ¼–½-inch layer of mortar over the damp surface of the stepping stone. The depth will depend on the size of your gems. The larger the gemstones, the deeper the mortar must be to hold them securely.

5. Preserving your pattern, carefully transfer the stones from the paper to the mortared surface of the stone, pressing them into the mortar so that they lie relatively evenly. Make sure that you leave a bit of space between gems for the grout.

6. Set the stone in a safe place to cure for at least 12 hours. Wash out the bucket you used for the mortar.

7. Put on the rubber gloves again. In the clean bucket, mix the grout according to the package directions. Again, do not mix the entire package. Mix only enough to cover the stone to a depth of approximately ½ inch, plus a little extra to be sure.

8. Scoop the grout onto the surface of the gems and smooth it out with the spatula. Make sure you work the grout in carefully between the

gems. Spread grout on the sides of the stone as well. When you are finished, use the spatula to smooth the top of the stone to remove any excess grout.

9. Using a damp sponge, gently wipe any remaining grout off the top of the stone and the gems. Wipe from the middle out and across to be sure that all the grout is smoothed down between the gems as well as washed off the tops of them. Rinse the sponge frequently to keep it clean and damp. Be careful not to wash or scrub away the grout between the gems.

10. Leave the stone to dry for approximately 24 hours. Polish it with a soft cloth.

Chapter 8

Become a Natural Healer

THERE ARE DEEP SPIRITUAL BENEFITS to walking the path of the green witch. By immersing yourself in the energy of the planet and its flora, you can achieve higher levels of consciousness, which will benefit all those you interact with and the environment in which you live.

Although one of the green witch's goals is to heal others, it is never wise to just give out teas or other preparations unless you are trained as a qualified herbalist. This is especially true if the preparation is intended for major or chronic problems. If someone comes to you complaining of a stomach upset or a headache, however, you can use your judgment and the folk knowledge you possess to suggest a treatment.

The Steps of Healing

Green witches are natural healers who seek to soothe the world around them. Healing is another form of rebalancing energies that have become disturbed. But healing cannot be rushed. Each step must be experienced in fullness and in time. This goes for healing the earth as well as yourself, other individuals, and the community. You have to learn from the process so that each step is thoroughly felt, understood, and completed. There are two steps to healing:

1. Cleansing and/or purifying of the negative presence
2. Replacing the negative presence with something positive

Many people focus on the first step and forget about the second. Nature abhors a vacuum, and what results from the first step is an empty space where the negative energy was and which new energy will rush to fill. The problem is that we do not always control what kind of energy fills that space. To gain control and finish the healing process properly, you can perform a blessing (which asks another entity or spirit to bestow positive energy) or channel positive energy yourself to strengthen the object or person being healed. Be wary, however, of channeling energy that has already been programmed until you know exactly what your subject needs. You may think your subject needs strength, but the need may be for something different. Filling the empty space with plain, unprogrammed, positive energy is safer. It allows the body to use it for whatever it requires.

To better understand the healing aspect of the green witch path, you can research healing deities of various cultures.

Brewing Healing Teas

A tea is a potion that can be consumed. Usually made with water, the basic technique for preparing a tea is by infusion if you're using leaves or flowers or decoction if you're using denser herbal material, such as roots, stems, twigs, or bark.

There are many teas available on the market today designed for certain therapeutic benefits such as stress relief, better sleep, headache relief, and so forth. While you can certainly use these commercial teas, when you create your own you know exactly what is going into them. You can also avoid herbs to which you are sensitive and use herbs you prefer.

Remember that taking anything internally without researching it can be dangerous. These recipes are not intended to be used as authoritative medical advice; they are offered here as folk wisdom.

All the following recipes may be made with fresh or dry herbs. If using fresh herbs, increase the amount of plant matter to 1 tablespoon per cup of boiling water for a single serving and make only enough for as many servings as you intend to prepare right away. Fresh blends cannot be stored.

MARSHMALLOW TEA

This tea is for the treatment of a sore throat or digestive problems. Its magical associations are protection and healing.

Makes 1 cup

- 1 tablespoon (⅔ ounce) dried chopped marshmallow root
- 1 cup water

1. Place marshmallow root in water.
2. Bring to a simmer, and simmer for 10 minutes.
3. Remove from heat and allow to steep for another 10 minutes.
4. Strain and drink.
5. Take as necessary throughout the day.

SAGE GARGLE

This tea is good for the treatment of colds and sore throat. Its magical associations are wisdom, protection, and purification.

Makes ½ cup

- ½ cup water
- 1 tablespoon dry sage (or 5–6 fresh sage leaves)

1. Boil the water and pour over the sage leaves.
2. Steep for 7 minutes.
3. Strain into a sterilized bottle and store in the fridge. To use, take 1 tablespoon and gargle for 1 minute. Do not swallow.

TONIC TEA

This tea is used for cleansing the blood and toning the digestive system. Its magical associations are protection and healing.

Makes approximately ¼ cup (2 ounces) of the tea blend; 1 tablespoon of the tea blend makes 1½ cups of tea

- 1 tablespoon rosemary
- 1 tablespoon yarrow
- 1 tablespoon horehound
- 1 teaspoon sage
- 1 large catnip leaf
- 1½ cups boiling water
- 1 tablespoon honey (optional)

1. Mix dry herbs in a small jar.
2. To brew, pour 1½ cups of boiling water over 1 tablespoon of the herbal mixture and steep for 7–10 minutes.

3. Strain and drink. If you find this tea too bitter, you may want to add a full teaspoon of honey.

DIGESTIVE TEA

This tea is good for the treatment of heartburn, upset stomach, and gas. Its magical association is prosperity.

1 teaspoon of the tea blend makes 1 cup of tea

- 1 part peppermint
- 1 part basil
- 1 part dill seed
- 1 cup boiling water

1. Mix dry herbs in a small jar.
2. To brew, pour 1 cup of boiling water over 1 teaspoon of the herbal blend.
3. Steep 7–10 minutes. Strain and drink.

COLD TEA

This tea is for the treatment of colds. Its magical associations are energy and healing.

1 teaspoon of the tea blend makes 1 cup of tea

- 1 part ginger
- 1 part elderflowers
- 1 part yarrow
- 1 cup boiling water

1. Mix dry herbs in a small jar.
2. To brew, pour 1 cup of boiling water over 1 teaspoon of the herbal blend.
3. Steep 5–7 minutes. Strain and drink.

BEDTIME TEA

This tea is good for aiding sleep. Its magical associations are peace, harmony, healing, love, and happiness.

1 teaspoon of the tea blend makes 1 cup of tea

- 1 part lavender
- 1 part catnip
- 1 part verbena
- 1 part chamomile
- 1 cup boiling water

1. Mix dry herbs in a small jar.
2. To brew, pour 1 cup of boiling water over 1 teaspoon of the herbal blend.
3. Steep 5–7 minutes. Strain and drink.

LOVE TEA

This tea is for relaxation and celebrating love. Its magical associations are love, happiness, peace, and harmony.

1 teaspoon of the tea blend makes 1 cup of tea

- 1 part rose petals
- 1 part lavender
- 1 part jasmine
- Pinch of cinnamon (optional)
- 1 cup boiling water

1. Mix herbs in a small jar.
2. To brew, pour 1 cup boiling water over 1 teaspoon of the herbal blend.
3. Steep 5–7 minutes. Strain and drink.

MENTAL FOCUS TEA

This tea is meant for mental focus, concentration, sharpening memory, and studying. Its magical uses are health, protection, happiness, and peace.

1 teaspoon of the tea blend makes 1 cup of tea

- 1 part rosemary
- ½ part spearmint
- 1 cup boiling water

1. Mix herbs in a small jar.
2. To brew, pour 1 cup boiling water over 1 teaspoon of the herbal blend.
3. Steep 5–7 minutes. Strain and drink.

Energy–Empowering Essential Oils

An oil is a handy way to carry the essence of an herb or other natural object. The basic ways to prepare an oil are by enfleurage or by maceration (see Chapter 7). If you prepare your own oils, they will carry the added benefit of already being attuned to you and your personal energy, although you should still empower them before use as you do with any supplies. Not everyone can prepare a full stock of as many oils as they would like to have. Two kinds of oils are generally available for purchase from shops: essential oils, which carry the pure essence of the plant in a carrier oil, and perfume oils, which are artificially scented.

Most green witches like to use as pure a product as possible in their work and will therefore choose an essential oil over a perfume oil. An essential oil is prepared directly from the original plant, which means that when you use it in magical or medicinal work it is guaranteed to carry the original energy of the plant along with its chemical benefits.

An essential oil is more expensive than perfume oil, but it will also be stronger; only a drop or two is necessary to involve the energy of the plant. The scent of a perfume oil is less accurate than in an essential oil and does not carry the plant's energy signature. Although irresponsible merchants sometimes attempt to sell artificial perfume oils as essential oils, the comparative prices are a good guide to identifying what is essential and what is perfume. When pure essential oils such as jasmine and rose sell for over $100 for a few milliliters, you can spot an artificial oil substitute when someone tries to sell it to you for $20. You can mix essential oils and perfume oils.

> Oils are generally used for anointing, but they can also be added to baths, potpourris, and sachets. Whether you create a personal blend or use a blend made from the following recipes, you can add a drop or two to any project you undertake for that magical purpose to add extra energy and power.

Blending oils is a wonderful activity that allows for experimentation and personal expression and also enhances your personal intuition. There will be times when you feel inspired to add a drop or two of a certain oil that wasn't in your original recipe. Do so, and make a note of the addition. When the oil has matured, perform an energy-sensing of it and write your observations in your journal under the new recipe. How has the energy changed? Use the oil and note your results. This is how recipes evolve over time and come to reflect the personal growth and understanding of the green witch.

PERSONAL OIL BLEND

Creating an oil specifically to represent yourself and your energy gives you a bottled essence that can be used for a multitude of purposes.

- Oils (your choice)
- Small dishes, bowls, or empty vials
- Container with tight-fitting lid for the final oil blend

1. The recipe for this blend is really up to you. Think about your favorite herbs, flowers, and trees. Think about the elements you resonate with. Think about the color of the plants the oils are derived from and the scent.

2. In your green witch notebook, make up a list of these elements. You don't have to limit them to oils you already have on hand. Also think about the emotions or goals you wish to include in your blend. Are you creative? Are you an excellent communicator? Are you a nurturer?

3. Next, look up correspondences for the plants on your list, then look up plants that correspond to the traits and goals on your list. Write this information in your journal.

4. Now start to narrow the list down. Use your intuition and consider the importance of what corresponds to what.

5. When you have a manageable list of between three and thirteen items, work out your proportions. How much of each oil? To begin, you may wish to blend everything in a proportion of one part each. You can also use one oil as a base and add only trace amounts of others. However you mix your personal oil, the way you put it together is up to you.

6. When you've worked out your proportions, take a look at your stock of oils. If you're missing oils, decide whether you will make them yourself (which will require time) or buy them. You will also need to

decide whether you will use essential oils or perfume oils. Remember, you can mix these oils together.

7. To blend your personal oil, measure out the appropriate proportions of your chosen oils and place each in an individual small dish or clean empty vial.

8. One by one, pour the oils into your chosen container. Swirl them together.

9. Empower the final oil blend by holding it in your hands and visualizing your personal energy flowing from your hands into the oil. Continue until you feel the oil has been fully empowered with your energy.

10. Cover and label your personal oil blend. Write down the date, the final ingredients, and the proportions in your green witch journal.

Following are oil recipes that you can use. They may also inspire you to create new recipes. Do not take these oils internally! Blend the oils by following steps 7 through 10 in the previous Personal Oil Blend recipe. If the recipe calls for an addition of herbal matter, add it last.

AWAKE AND ALIVE OIL

The magical associations of this oil are happiness, health, protection, and energy.

- 1 part rosemary
- 1 part mint
- 1 part orange
- ½ part lemon
- ½ part thyme

PATIENCE

The magical associations of this oil are peace, harmony, and love.

- 1 part rose
- 1 part lavender
- 1 part pine

CLEAR DECISIONS

This oil's magical associations are clear thinking, harmony, health, and protection.

- 1 part pine
- 1 part rosemary
- 1 part sage

PROSPERITY

The magical associations of this oil are movement and energy.

- 1 part mint
- 1 part basil
- 1 part cinnamon
- 1 part pine

HEALTH

This oil's magical associations are health, communication, and strength.

- 1 part thyme
- 1 part eucalyptus
- 1 part pine
- 1 part ginger

PEACE

The magical associations of this oil are meditation, spirituality, and harmony.

- 1 part violet
- 1 part lavender
- 1 part jasmine
- 1 part sandalwood

PROTECTION

This oil's magical associations are protection, wisdom, and purification.

- 1 part sage
- 1 part sandalwood
- 1 part angelica
- 1 clove
- Pinch of salt

LOVE

The magical associations of this oil are love and harmony.

- 1 part rose
- 1 part jasmine
- ½ part geranium
- ¼ part vanilla

Regenerating Baths and Bath Salts

A bath is a magical thing. Water itself is a healing and soothing element, and when you add a potion to it you can create a wide range of effects.

To avoid having leaves and stems and other little bits of green matter floating around in your tub and clogging the drain, you can make an infusion or a decoction and pour it into your bathwater. You can also put a couple of spoonfuls of an herbal blend inside an old sock or stocking, tie a knot in it, and toss it in under the running water as you fill the tub. The result in an infusion brewed directly in your bath. Remove the sock or stocking before you get in, or leave it to further strengthen the infusion while you bathe. When you remove it, hang it up and allow it to dry, then undo the knot and turn it inside out to brush away the dried herbal matter. You can reuse the sock or stocking. Alternatively, you can make a reusable bath sachet by sewing two washcloths together on three sides, leaving the top open. Sew 12 inches of ribbon or string to one side seam about one third of the way down. Place your spoonfuls of dried or fresh herbs inside (no more than ½ cup), then gather the open end and tie the pouch closed by wrapping the ribbon or string around it firmly and tying a bow. You can hang this bath sachet under the faucet as the water runs or toss it in and allow it to soak.

You can also use oils in your bath. If you are using essential oils, make sure you use only three drops total. Any more can irritate your skin or overwhelm your system. Remember, essential oils are concentrated extracts that carry chemicals. It's easy to overdose on them. If you prefer to bathe with lots of oil, blend those three drops into a quarter cup of a carrier oil, such as jojoba or sweet almond oil, then pour all the oil into your bath. I recommend that you do this with both essential and perfume oils because your skin may be sensitive to both. Adding a few drops to a carrier oil makes for a safer bathing experience.

For a different sort of bath, blend the drops of oil into 1 cup of milk and pour that into the running water.

BATH SALTS

Bath salts are a lovely way to relax and absorb magical energy at the same time. Salt is a naturally purifying substance that also helps relax tense muscles. When a bath salt recipe calls for salt, however, it doesn't mean table salt. Epsom salts, sea salt, kosher salt, or a combination should be used. You can buy sea salt at natural food stores and many grocery stores. You can buy kosher salt at grocery stores or Jewish specialty shops. Epsom salts can be found at your pharmacy.

> Other additives to homemade bath salts include powdered milk, vegetable food coloring, powdered herbs, and crystals or stones. If you add oil, you have a salt scrub.

You can blend and store your bath salts in mason jars, but remember that the salt can corrode the metal lids. Look for jars with glass lids fitted with plastic seals, jars with snap-down lids, or jars with cork tops. Never store bath salts in a metal tin or it will rust, and be aware that a plastic container will tend to absorb the scent of the salts, which makes it difficult to reuse.

In general, use 1 tablespoon to 1/4 cup of these salts in your bath. If you prefer a lot of salt in your bath, increase the amount slowly to make sure you don't irritate your skin or system.

BASIC BATH SALT RECIPE

Use this recipe as a basis for your own magical bath salts. You can use any combination of sea salt, Epsom salts, and kosher salt.

Makes 4 cups (32 ounces)

- 2 cups sea salt or other salts
- 2 cups baking soda
- Glass jar with tight-fitting lid, large enough to hold 32 ounces

1. Combine ingredients in blender or food processor. Blend until combined and reduced to a fine powder.
2. Store in a tightly lidded jar.
3. To use, pour ½ cup of the salts into the bath under running water.

To this basic recipe you can add any or all of the following:

- 3–5 drops of essential oil(s)
- 2 teaspoons of finely ground dried herbs
- 1–3 drops of food coloring
- If your skin tends to be dry, add 1 teaspoon liquid glycerin (available in drugstores) to moisturize your skin.
- 1 part finely ground oatmeal
- ½ part finely ground almonds

PROSPERITY BATH SALTS

Use this recipe when you feel you need to boost your personal prosperity energy.

Makes 2½ cups (20 ounces)

- 1 cup sea salt
- 1 cup Epsom salts

- Glass jar with tight-fitting lid, large enough to hold 20 ounces
- 3 drops orange oil
- 2 drops cinnamon oil OR 1 teaspoon ground cinnamon
- ¼ cup ground mint leaves
- 3 drops green vegetable food coloring (optional)

1. Place the salts in a blender or food processor and blend to combine and reduce to a fine powder. Pour the salts into the jar and cap it. Shake to combine the salts.

2. Open the jar again. Add the drops of oil and the ground herbs. Cap the jar and shake well to blend.

3. If using food coloring, open the jar and add 3 drops. Cap and shake well to blend. Be aware that a little food coloring goes a long way; don't add much. If you want the color darker, add 1–2 more drops and blend again. The color is added simply to enhance the prosperity energy of the other ingredients. If you associate another color with prosperity, then by all means substitute it.

4. To use, pour ½ cup of the salts into your bath under running water.

MILK BATHS

There's something remarkably luxurious about adding milk to your bathwater. Milk has a wonderfully softening action on the skin. Do not, however, use milk baths if you are sensitive to dairy products.

The simplest recipe for a milk bath is to take 1 cup of whole milk (don't use skim or even partially skim milk) and pour it into your bathwater. For extra softening action, add 1 tablespoon of honey to the cup of milk and swirl it about to disperse it before pouring it into the water. If you like, you can warm the milk up first to help blend in the honey: heat the honey-milk mixture in the microwave for 1 minute. You can also add a few drops of oil to the warm milk before pouring it into your bath. Swirling to combine the oil with the milk helps disperse the oil throughout the bathwater, instead of just letting it float on the surface of the water.

If you want to make milk bath powders ahead of time and store them, use powdered milk. When you add a scoop to your bathwater, it dissolves and functions just like fresh milk.

OATMEAL MILK BATH

The combination of oatmeal, a known skin softener, and milk in this bath blend makes for a deliciously soothing soak. Try it if you're sunburned or to soften rough skin. You can also add herbs or a couple of drops of oil to the following recipe.

Makes 4 cups (32 ounces)

- 1 cup cornstarch
- 2 cups milk powder
- 1 cup dry oatmeal
- Glass jar with tight-fitting lid, large enough to hold 32 ounces

1. Place all the ingredients in a food processor or blender. Blend to combine until reduced to a fine powder. Pour into jar.
2. To use, sprinkle ½ cup of the dry bath blend under the tap while running your bath.

HERBAL MILK BATH

This basic and simple milk bath is an excellent base for any herbal addition, making it adaptable to any magical need. For extra softening, you can use the Oatmeal Milk Bath as a base.

Makes 3 cups (24 ounces)

- 1 cup cornstarch
- 2 cups milk powder
- 2 tablespoons dry herbs
- Glass jar with tight-fitting lid, large enough to hold 24 ounces

1. Place all ingredients in a blender or food processor. Blend until combined and reduced to a fine powder. Pour into jar.
2. To use, add ½ cup of powder to bath under running water.

Here are some suggested herbal blends to add to milk baths:

- **Winter Energy Bath:** nutmeg, cinnamon, pinch of ginger
- **Summer Garden Bath:** lavender, roses, verbena, pinch of orange zest
- **Autumn Bronze Bath:** poppy, nutmeg, sandalwood
- **Spring Dawn Bath:** lavender, jasmine, apple blossom

Make Restorative Elixirs

Elixirs can be used to anoint objects, and also people, as long as they have not been made with toxic components. Some may be consumed as well. Elixirs can also be used like objects: they can be brewed and bottled, then placed somewhere to work their effect upon the surroundings.

STONE ELIXIRS

Steep a stone in water for a measured amount of time in sunlight or moonlight. You may leave the stone in the liquid and renew the fluid as necessary. Make sure the stone is scrubbed clean and rinsed well before you use it. Also make sure you have cleansed the stone of any foreign energy by any of the methods described in Chapter 5.

COLOR ELIXIRS

Pour water into a clean colored glass jar or bottle, then leave in sunlight or moonlight for a specific amount of time. The light passing through the colored glass will imbue the liquid inside with the energy of the color. People often drink color elixirs if they feel they are lacking the energy of that certain color.

If you cannot find a jar or bottle in the color you need, take a piece of colored paper and wrap it around the outside of a clear glass bottle or jar. Pour the water into the bottle and leave it for one complete moon cycle.

Chapter 9

Green Witch Kitchen Recipes

WE MUST REMEMBER that eating is a sacred act. In consuming a food, be it animal based or plant based, we forge a connection with nature, the source of nourishment. By taking this nourishment into our bodies, we also honor nature's presence within our lives, and acknowledge our place within the natural order. Harvesting and preparing food are also sacred acts that we tend to compress into the smallest amount of time possible in order to free ourselves up for other things. When we understand that the act of preparing food is the conscious weaving together of various energies to achieve a specific goal, and that eating with intention leads to our assimilation of those energies, we understand that preparing and eating food with awareness give these actions another dimension of meaning. This chapter explores the energies associated with different foods and offers some ideas on how to combine them in delicious recipes.

Tap Into the Energies of Fruits

Fruit is a plant's method of reproducing itself and carries an energy based in fertility and abundance. All fruit carries seeds, which are the beginning of life. Whether we consume the seeds or not, their fertile energy permeates the whole fruit. Fruit is also an excellent way to consume seasonal energy, for different fruits appear at different points of the seasonal cycle.

MAGICAL ASSOCIATIONS OF FRUIT

Use this list of correspondences to help you select your own combinations of fruit for salads, pies, and smoothies:

- **Apple:** health, longevity, love
- **Pear:** health, prosperity, love
- **Orange:** joy, health, purification
- **Lemon:** purification, protection, health
- **Lime:** happiness, purification, healing
- **Grape:** prosperity, fertility
- **Kiwi:** fertility, love
- **Banana:** fertility, strength
- **Mango:** spirituality, happiness
- **Peach:** spirituality, fertility, love, harmony
- **Pineapple:** prosperity, luck, protection
- **Plum:** love, tranquility
- **Melons:** love, peace
- **Strawberries:** love, peace, happiness, luck
- **Raspberries:** strength, courage, healing
- **Blueberries:** tranquility, peace, protection, prosperity
- **Blackberries:** prosperity, protection, abundance
- **Cranberries:** protection, healing

FRUIT RECIPES

Fruit is so delicious on its own that it rarely needs any complicated preparation. The following recipes take advantage of this simplicity.

FRUIT BOWL

This simple recipe gathers seasonal fruit into a bowl for display and consumption, making it part craft, part spell, part recipe. Include nuts for visual interest and to add a touch of fertility and abundance to your display. Assemble a selection of seasonal fruit, for example:

- Spring: strawberries, cantaloupe, cherries
- Summer: oranges, grapefruit, lemons, limes, peaches, nectarines, plums, berries
- Autumn: apples, plums, peaches, grapes
- Winter: nuts, apples, oranges

1. Wash fruit and pat dry with clean cloth or paper towel.
2. Arrange fruit in a large glass bowl in a pleasing display. Use as an offering during a seasonal ritual, as a centerpiece, or as breakfast or dessert.

PROSPERITY FRUIT SALAD

This seasonal breakfast or dessert gathers together fruit associated with prosperity and abundance. Choose as much or as little of each fruit as you like.

- Fresh pineapple chunks
- Blueberries
- Cherries, pitted and sliced in half
- Grapes, sliced in half, seeds removed
- Apples, diced

- Pears, diced
- 1 teaspoon lemon juice
- ¼ cup sugar

1. Wash, dry, and cut fruit into appropriately sized pieces.
2. Combine fruit in a bowl. Sprinkle lemon juice over the fruit.
3. Sprinkle sugar over the fruit and leave to rest for 1 hour.

FRUIT DRINKS

There is something remarkably satisfying about making a fruit beverage. Once all the preparation is complete, you can enjoy the drink without getting your fingers sticky. There are two basic kinds of smoothie, those made with fruit and juice and those made with fruit and milk, cream, yogurt, or ice cream. These easy-to-make beverages combine various fruits to create a delicious potion for prosperity, health, or love.

Like fruit, dairy products are magically associated with abundance, love, and comfort, so if dairy energy supports your magical goal, then include milk or cream or other dairy products in your smoothie recipe.

Basic fruit juices to include in your nondairy smoothies include apple, pear, and white grape. You can also use cranberry and orange, but these have a stronger taste and may not complement your chosen fruit blend. As you experiment with smoothies, you may wish to add one teaspoon of lemon or lime juice to your creation to enhance the flavor.

NONDAIRY FRUIT SMOOTHIE

This recipe makes one serving but can be increased to serve more. If you choose to use watermelon as one of the fruits, omit the juice in your smoothie recipe or it will become too thin.

- Your choice of fruit (see previous list of fruit for correspondences)
- ¼ cup fruit juice (apple, pear, or white grape)
- ¼–1 teaspoon sugar, or to taste (optional)
- Fruit for garnish

1. Peel, seed, and dice the fruit.
2. Place the diced fruit in the blender with the juice and sugar, if using.
3. Cover and blend until smooth.
4. Pour into glass. Garnish with fruit on rim or set the glass on a saucer or small plate and arrange a bit of fruit around the base as a garnish.

DAIRY FRUIT SMOOTHIE

This version of the fruit smoothie incorporates yogurt as one of the ingredients. For a thinner drink, use milk; for a thicker, sweeter, more dessert-like treat, use ice cream. For nondairy milks, try almond milk or soy milk, which both have a sweet flavor. (Omit sugar if using nondairy milks.)

- ¾–1 cup fruit of your choice
- ¼ cup plain yogurt
- 1 teaspoon–1 tablespoon sugar (optional)
- Fruit for garnish (optional)

1. Peel, seed, and dice the fruit.
2. Place fruit in the blender with the yogurt and sugar, if using.
3. Blend until smooth.

4. Pour into glass. Garnish glass with fruit, or place on saucer or small plate and garnish around the base of the glass.

5. If the drink is too thick, stir in a bit of milk. If it isn't thick enough, return it to the blender and add more fruit.

Integrate the Power of Flowers

Although we usually think of herbs when we think of flavorings, flowers can also be used in cooking and baking to provide a wonderfully subtle flavor. You can add whole flowers or petals to your food, but often you want the flavor without the actual plant matter. Syrups, waters, and preserved petals are all handy ways to use floral flavorings. For magical associations of flowers, see Chapter 5.

A surprising number of flowers are edible. Explore the flowers available in your area to discover which may be safely eaten by checking the botanical name of your local varieties against a reliable book. In general, the following are safe to eat, as long as they have not been treated with pesticides or grown in questionable soil:

- Angelica
- Apple blossoms
- Basil
- Bee balm
- Borage
- Calendula
- Chamomile
- Chicory
- Dandelion
- Elderflower
- Lavender

- Lilac
- Linden
- Lovage
- Mint
- Nasturtium
- Pansy
- Red clover
- Violet

CANDIED FLOWERS

This is a lovely way to preserve blossoms for future use. Use them to decorate cakes and desserts or as an offering in a ritual.

Eggs are associated with prosperity, healing, protection, and health. Sugar is associated with love and happiness. The edible flower that you choose to candy will carry its own specific energy. I suggest such blossoms as rose petals (love, happiness), sweet violets (peace, harmony), nasturtiums (protection, healing), pansies (love, happiness), and sprigs of lavender (peace, happiness, harmony). Some herbs such as rosemary also make interesting candied sprigs for a slightly savory addition to desserts with citrus flavors. Experiment!

BASIC CANDIED FLOWERS

- 2 cups assorted organic edible flowers
- ½ cup superfine sugar (or fruit sugar)
- ¼ cup egg whites (3 large egg whites), beaten
- Tweezers
- Small paintbrush
- Spoon

- Bowls
- Waxed paper
- Airtight container

1. Gently wash and dry the flowers. You may separate the individual petals from the stems or cut the whole flower off the stem. Discard the stem and leaves.
2. Place the sugar in one bowl, the beaten egg whites in another bowl.
3. Pick up the flower or petal with the tweezers. Using the paintbrush, paint a thin layer of egg white on all surfaces of the flower or petal.
4. Gently place the blossom in the bowl of sugar. Using the spoon, sprinkle more sugar over the flower to coat it completely.
5. Using the tweezers, remove the flower from the bowl and place it gently on the waxed paper.
6. Continue with the rest of the flowers.
7. Sprinkle the blossoms on the waxed paper with more sugar, if necessary. Allow to dry until hardened, at least 8 hours. If your environment is humid, place the flowers on a foil-covered baking sheet instead of waxed paper, and place in a barely warm oven (150°F) with the door cracked open for approximately 2 hours. The flowers must be completely dry before you pack them carefully between layers of waxed paper in the airtight container.

FLORAL WATERS

Although floral waters can be used in baking where any recipe calls for water, they're also known as lovely facial splashes. Rose water is perhaps the best known, although you can make several variations with edible flowers. Think of the magical associations for whatever purpose you intend to use the water, and choose the flowers accordingly. Try chilling a floral water in a spray bottle, then spritzing it on your face and body as a wonderful way to cool off in the summer. You can also blend floral waters. Prepare each water separately, one flower per water, then combine the floral waters into new blends. For example, try blending lavender and violet waters for a light, refreshing way to cool off before bed in the summertime, or blend orange and a touch of mint for a winter spray. Remember to use only flowers that have not been sprayed with chemicals.

If you wish to store the floral water for longer than one week for future use, freeze the water in a clean ice cube tray. Pop the frozen cubes out of the tray and store them in clearly labeled zip-top bags.

You can increase or decrease the following recipe as long as you retain the proportions. If you make a floral water and you aren't pleased with the results, increase or decrease the number of petals the next time you make it. Remember, floral waters aren't meant to be strong infusions or teas; there should be just the barest hint of floral scent and flavor.

ROSE GERANIUM WATER

This recipe uses the fragrant leaves of the scented rose geranium. You can use this water to replace water called for in any recipe. Rose geranium is magically associated with love and peace.

- 3 large rose geranium leaves, washed
- Glass jar with lid (1 pint or half-quart size)
- 2 cups boiling water

1. Place rose geranium leaves in the jar and pour the boiling water over them. Allow to steep until cool.

2. Remove leaves. Store floral water in the refrigerator up to 1 week.

FLOWER SYRUPS

Floral syrups make a lovely substitute for honey to sweeten tea. They are also a delicate treat poured over vanilla ice cream and angel food cake for a simple dessert.

VIOLET SYRUP

Make this syrup with fresh-picked sweet violets. Remember to use unsprayed flowers only and be sure to wash and dry them well. Violets encourage harmony and peace, while the sugar sweetens any situation. The magical associations of this syrup are peace, harmony, and happiness.

Makes approximately 1 quart of syrup

- 2 cups water, divided
- 2 cups violet flowers
- 2 deep glass or china bowls
- Strainer
- Cheesecloth
- Heavy pot (try to use glass if you can; some people think the metal can affect the taste)
- 3 cups granulated sugar
- 1½ tablespoons lime juice
- Clean glass bottle or jar with cap
- Sparkling water or club soda

1. Boil 1 cup of water.

2. Place violet petals in a deep glass bowl and cover them with the boiling water. Allow to steep for 24 hours.

3. Line the strainer with cheesecloth and pour the violet infusion through it into the second bowl. Wring out the violet flowers to obtain the last of the infusion. Discard flowers.

4. In the pot, bring sugar, lime juice, and the second cup of water to a boil. Boil carefully until it thickens slightly.

5. Add violet water. Bring mixture to a boil and boil until thick once more, 5–10 minutes.

6. Remove from heat and pour into a clean bottle or jar; cap, label and date. Store in the refrigerator.

7. To serve, spoon approximately ¼ cup of syrup into the bottom of a highball glass, and pour sparkling water over it. Stir to disperse the syrup. Add ice. Adjust the amount of syrup to water according to your taste.

You can also add the syrup to a sweet base such as ginger ale or lemon-lime soda, in which case adjust the amount of syrup you use down to 1 tablespoon (or to taste). Try adding a drizzle of syrup to sweeten your coffee or tea, or to warm milk for a pleasant bedtime treat.

FLOWER SUGARS

Delicately flavored floral sugars make a delicious treat to stir into tea.

LAVENDER SUGAR

This sugar is different from an infused sugar in that it actually combines the herbal matter with the sugar itself. That is, the flowers are not sifted out. The magical associations of this recipe are peace, harmony, love, and happiness.

- 1 part lavender flowers (strip off the stems)
- 1 part granulated sugar
- Jar with secure lid

1. Place lavender flowers and sugar in a blender.
2. Process for 3 minutes, or until the flowers and sugar are in tiny pieces and well blended.
3. Place in a jar with a secure lid and store for up to 1 month.

Craft Vinegars for Potency

We are all familiar with infused herbal vinegars, which are easy to prepare. Simply chop or lightly bruise a handful of whatever fresh herb you wish to infuse and place the herb in a glass jar with a tight-fitting lid. Cover the herbal matter with wine, cider, or rice vinegar, seal, and let it rest for at least two to three weeks in the refrigerator, shaking it periodically. Strain out the herbal matter (or it will become bitter). Taste. If the flavor is not strong enough, add a new batch of chopped or bruised fresh herb to the infusion, cap, and let it rest for another week. Check weekly. When the desired flavor has been obtained, strain out the herbal matter. (If the flavor is not strong enough by three weeks of infusing the second batch of herbs, strain them out and replace with a new batch.)

Fruit vinegars are less well known but are made by the same method:

1. Dice or lightly crush approximately 1 cup of fruit and place it in a glass container with a tight-fitting lid. (Do not add too much fruit, or the natural sugars will counter the vinegar's natural acidic qualities.)

2. Cover the fruit with cider or wine vinegar. Seal the container and allow it to steep in the refrigerator until the taste is to your liking. Shake the container periodically.

3. Strain the fruit out when the strength of the infusion is to your taste.

4. Store in the refrigerator.

Fruit vinegars make lovely dressings for salads and refreshing additions to marinades.

Add Sweetness with Infused Sugars

Flavored sugars can be used in the place of any regular sugar when baking or to sweeten tea. Try it over granola or muesli at breakfast or sprinkle it over buttered toast for a sweet treat. Add a teaspoonful of infused sugar to whipped cream as you beat it for a gentle floral flavor to enhance fresh berries or cake. To make a flavored sugar try this method:

1. Layer clean dry herbs or spices with granulated sugar and cap tightly.

2. Allow to mature for at least three weeks. If the flavorings you have chosen are strong (for example, cinnamon or clove), check on the flavor of the sugar after two weeks. If they are very delicate, you may wish to leave the herbs longer to strengthen the flavor.

Do not use powdered herbs or spices for this project. Use whole or cracked seeds or fruit. For example, insert whole cloves, or break up a cinnamon stick and push the smaller pieces of the stick into the sugar.

For floral sugars it's important to separate the petals and make sure that no green matter remains attached to them. You may wish to snip away the white end of the petal (the pistil) where it joins the stem. Make certain that the flower you have chosen is an edible one. Although you will sift out the petals when you are done, the oils and flavor of the petal will remain, and as interesting as the flower smells, you cannot judge the safety of its taste by such means.

Here are some recommended flowers and herbs to use alone or in combination to create delicious infused sugars:

- Lavender
- Vanilla bean
- Rose
- Violet
- Mint leaves
- Orange blossom
- Scented geranium

INFUSED SUGAR

Do not substitute dried spices such as cinnamon or clove for the herbs in this recipe; the resulting flavor of the sugar will be too intense. For a sugar made with dried spices, see the following recipe for Spiced Sugar.

Makes 1 cup of infused herbal or floral sugar

- Clean, dry glass jar with tight-fitting lid
- 1 cup granulated sugar
- 1 cup clean, dry, fresh flowers or herbs

1. Pour ¼ cup of sugar into the bottom of the glass jar.
2. Spread ¼ cup of herbs or flower petals on top of the sugar.
3. Pour another ¼ cup of sugar over the herbs.
4. Repeat with herbal layer, followed by sugar layer, another herbal layer, and a sugar layer. Leave about a ½ inch of room at the top of the jar.
5. Cap the jar securely and shake the mixture to disperse the herbal matter throughout the sugar.
6. Place the sugar jar in a cool, dark place and allow it to sit for 3 weeks to 1 month before using.
7. If you intend to bake or cook with infused sugar, sift out the herbal matter. If you leave the herbs or flowers in the sugar, remember that the longer it sits, the more flavorful it becomes. As you use the sugar, fill the jar with more unflavored sugar. Cap and shake it and it will take on the fragrance of the flowers in the jar.
8. If you live in a humid environment, keep a close eye on the herbs or flowers, as they may begin to mold or rot. If this happens, then the sugar must be thrown out. To avoid this, make certain that all the herbs and flowers are completely dry when you begin, and sift the plant matter out of the sugar once the flavor reaches the intensity you prefer.

SPICED SUGAR

This recipe creates a lovely spiced sugar suitable for baking, flavoring coffee or strong black tea, and adding to crumble toppings of coffee cakes or fruit crisps. If you make a sugar with only one spice (such as cinnamon sugar), you can simply snap a cinnamon stick in several places and insert it into a small jar of sugar. Leave this jar in a cool, dry place to mature for at least 2 weeks. As you use the sugar, replace it with fresh granulated sugar and shake it.

- 1 cup granulated sugar
- 1 tablespoon ground cinnamon
- 1 teaspoon ground cloves
- 1 teaspoon nutmeg
- 2 teaspoons ground ginger
- Clean, dry glass jar with tight lid

1. In a small bowl, blend the spices together.
2. Pour ¼ cup of sugar in the bottom of the jar.
3. Sprinkle ¼ of the spice blend on top.
4. Cover the spice blend with another ¼ cup of sugar. Repeat layering, topping with the final ¼ cup of sugar. Leave approximately ½ inch of room at the top of the jar before capping securely.
5. Shake the mixture to blend it.
6. Place the jar of sugar in a cool, dark place and allow it to sit for 2 weeks before using.
7. If you do not have ground cinnamon or cloves, crack a cinnamon stick in several places and add that in with a clove or two per layer of spice. Remember to sift the sugar before using it. Add a scored vanilla bean to the spiced sugar for an even more delicious treat!

Boost Health with Vegetables

Like fruit, a vegetable is a plant's visible seed container, and vegetables thus carry the magical associations of cycles and fertility. When you cook, therefore, you can choose your vegetables for their seasonal associations and eat them to attune to the seasonal energy. You can also choose them for their magical associations.

Here's a brief list of common vegetables and their magical associations:

- **Garlic:** healing, protection, banishing, purification
- **Onion:** protection, exorcism, healing, prosperity
- **Lettuce:** fertility, peace, harmony, protection
- **Carrots:** fertility, health
- **Peas:** love, abundance
- **Cucumber:** fertility, healing, harmony
- **Potatoes:** fertility, protection, abundance
- **Celery:** love, tranquility, concentration
- **Squash:** abundance, harmony
- **Mushroom:** strength, courage, healing, protection
- **Leek:** protection, harmony
- **Cauliflower:** protection, fertility
- **Broccoli:** protection, abundance
- **Beans:** love, family, protection
- **Cabbage:** protection, prosperity
- **Tomato:** protection, love

SOUPS

Soup is a wonderful way to use vegetables. A main dish of soup with a hearty bread can be a filling way to enjoy these healthy foods. Here are a handful of vegetable-based soup recipes for various seasons.

GAZPACHO

This chilled vegetable soup is a refreshing summer solstice treat or a pleasant accompaniment to grilled meats. Magical associations for this soup include prosperity, health, love, protection, peace, and harmony. This recipe is a green witch's dream, for it covers almost all seven basic areas of her focus. Green peppers are associated with prosperity; cucumber is associated with peace, harmony, and health; tomatoes are associated with love and health; celery is associated with peace; onions and garlic are associated with protection and health; and avocados are associated with love.

Serves 4–6

- 2 large green bell peppers, cored, seeded, and diced
- 1 large cucumber, peeled and chopped
- 2 pounds tomatoes, cored and diced
- 1 celery stalk, chopped
- 1 medium onion, peeled and chopped
- 2 garlic cloves, peeled
- 1 medium avocado, chopped (optional)
- 1 teaspoon salt
- ¼ teaspoon freshly ground black pepper
- Pinch of basil
- Pinch of parsley

- ⅓ cup olive oil
- 1 tablespoon lemon juice
- ¼ cup red wine vinegar
- 2 (12–15 ounce) cans tomato juice or V8 juice

1. In a blender, combine first seven ingredients in small batches and blend until smooth.
2. Pour into a large bowl. Add the remaining ingredients and stir well to combine.
3. Cover and chill for at least 5 hours or overnight. Stir well and taste for seasoning before serving. Adjust as necessary.
4. Serve in bowls or large mugs. Garnish soup as desired with croutons, sour cream or yogurt, or parsley.

APPLE, ALMOND, AND CURRY SOUP

A refreshing twist on standard soup, this is a lovely meal to serve around the autumn equinox. Magical associations for this soup include health and healing, prosperity, and protection. Apples are associated with health, healing, love, protection, and immortality. Almonds carry the energy of prosperity and healing. Curry is associated with protection.

Serves 4–6

- ¼ cup butter
- 1 medium onion, peeled and finely chopped
- 1½ pounds apples, cored, peeled, and diced
- 6 tablespoons ground almonds
- 4 cups chicken or vegetable stock
- ½ teaspoon curry powder
- ¼ teaspoon salt

- ¼ teaspoon freshly ground black pepper, or to taste
- ½ cup light cream, plain yogurt, or almond milk
- Toasted sliced almonds for garnish

1. Melt butter in a large saucepan. Add onion and cook gently until softened (about 5 minutes). Add the diced apples and stir gently for 2–3 minutes.

2. Sprinkle ground almonds over the apple and onion mixture and stir for another 1–2 minutes.

3. Pour in the stock and curry powder and bring to a boil. Add salt and pepper to taste.

4. Reduce heat to low. Cover and simmer for 20 minutes. Apples should be tender.

5. Remove from heat and allow to cool slightly. Pour the soup into the blender or food processor and blend until smooth.

6. Pour soup through a strainer into a clean pan. Add cream, yogurt, or almond milk and stir until blended. Taste for seasoning and adjust if necessary. If soup is too thick, add a bit more stock. Reheat gently.

7. Serve hot, garnished with a few slices of toasted sliced almonds, with an additional pinch of curry powder on top if you desire.

TOMATO SOUP

Tomatoes have traditionally been associated with love and protection. They're also bursting with vitamins, which makes them an ideal fruit to use for improving health. Basil is associated with love, protection, and prosperity, while cheese is associated with love, joy, and spirituality. Magical associations for this soup include prosperity, health and healing, and love.

Serves 4–6

- 2 tablespoons olive oil
- 1 medium onion, peeled and diced
- 2 garlic cloves, peeled and finely chopped
- 1–2 tablespoons fresh pesto (optional)
- 4 cups chopped fresh tomatoes
- 2 cups chicken or vegetable stock
- ¼ teaspoon salt
- ¼ teaspoon freshly ground black pepper, or to taste
- Shredded fresh basil for garnish
- 2 tablespoons grated Asiago or mozzarella cheese for garnish

1. Heat the oil in a large saucepan. Add the onion, garlic, and pesto (if using). Cook gently for 5 minutes over medium heat until onion is soft.

2. Add the tomatoes and the stock. Stir well and bring to a boil. Add salt and pepper.

3. Reduce heat to low. Cover and simmer gently, stirring occasionally, for 15–20 minutes.

4. Remove from heat and allow soup to cool slightly. Pour into a food processor or blender and blend in batches until smooth. Strain into a clean pot to remove any remaining lumps.

5. Return soup to the stove and reheat gently. Taste for seasoning and adjust if necessary. Add more stock if the soup is too thick.

6. Serve hot in bowls. Sprinkle with shredded fresh basil, a pinch of grated Asiago or mozzarella cheese, and a pinch of freshly ground pepper.

CARROT, CORIANDER, AND ORANGE SOUP

This is a wonderful late summer or early autumn soup. Magical associations for this soup include health and happiness. Carrots are associated with health and vital energy, while oranges are associated with happiness and health. Both are a bright orange color, which is associated with health, success, and solar energy. The coriander in this recipe carries the energy of love and active, vital energy.

Serves 4–6

- 3 tablespoons olive oil
- 1 medium onion, peeled and roughly chopped
- 1½ pounds carrots, peeled and thinly sliced
- 2–3 tablespoons ground coriander
- ¼ teaspoon salt
- ¼ teaspoon freshly ground black pepper, or to taste
- 4 cups chicken or vegetable stock
- ¼ cup freshly squeezed orange juice
- Thin strips orange zest (optional for garnish)
- Crushed coriander seeds (optional for garnish)

1. Heat the oil in a large stockpot. Add the onion and cook gently for 5 minutes or until soft.
2. Add carrots, coriander, salt, and pepper to taste. Cover and heat gently for 5 minutes to soften carrots, shaking the pan from time to time to prevent them from sticking.
3. Pour in stock and stir. Bring to a boil. Lower the heat, and cover the pot. Simmer gently for 30 minutes or until carrots are very tender.

4. Remove from heat and allow to cool slightly. Pour into a blender or food processor and blend in small batches until smooth. Strain soup into a clean pot to remove any remaining lumps.

5. Add the orange juice to the soup and reheat gently. Add more stock if the soup is too thick. Taste for seasoning and adjust if necessary.

6. Serve hot in bowls. If desired, garnish with strips of orange zest and crushed coriander seeds.

ONION SOUP

Onion soup is a delicious way to warm up in the winter. Magical associations of this soup include health and protection. Onions carry the energy of protection from evil and harm as well as good health. They are also an excellent food to consume to boost the immune system to fight illness. Parsley is associated with protection, prosperity, and fertility.

Serves 4–6

- 6 tablespoons butter
- 4–6 large white onions, peeled and chopped
- 3 tablespoons brown sugar
- 2 tablespoons flour
- 4 cups chicken or vegetable stock
- 2 tablespoons chopped fresh parsley
- ¼ teaspoon salt, or to taste
- ¼ teaspoon freshly ground black pepper, or to taste
- ¼ cup sherry or port (optional)
- Baguette or croutons for garnish
- 1 cup grated mozzarella cheese for garnish
- Chopped parsley for garnish

1. Melt the butter in a large saucepan. Add onions and brown sugar and cook over medium-high heat, stirring constantly, for 15 minutes or until sticky and caramel-brown. Remove from heat.

2. Stir in flour. Slowly add stock, stirring constantly. Return to heat and bring to a boil, stirring regularly. Add parsley and salt and pepper to taste.

3. Cover and simmer gently for 20 minutes, stirring occasionally.

4. Add the sherry or port (if using). Taste and adjust seasoning if required.

5. Serve hot in bowls. Garnish with a slice of toasted baguette or croutons, sprinkled with grated cheese and chopped parsley. If desired, place bowls on a baking sheet and place under the broiler for 1 minute to melt cheese completely.

Incorporate the Goodness of Grains

In general, grains—wheat, barley, rice, and corn—represent security, abundance, fertility, cycles, and prosperity. Here are two recipes for side dishes based on grains. They both incorporate herbs and cheese, which is magically associated with love and health. You may adjust the herbs to those of your preference.

CHEESE AND HERB RICE

Rice is magically associated with fertility, prosperity, and abundance, which is one of the reasons it has traditionally been thrown at wedded couples. This recipe makes a good side dish to serve with a sturdy meat or heavy vegetable dish.

Serves 4 as a side dish

- 1 cup uncooked white rice
- 1¾–2 cups chicken or vegetable stock

- ½ cup shredded Cheddar cheese
- 1 small onion, peeled and grated
- 2 large eggs, beaten
- ¼ cup butter
- ½ cup mixed fresh chopped herbs (such as rosemary, parsley, thyme, oregano, chives)
- 1½ cups milk

1. Preheat oven to 250°F.
2. In a medium saucepan, bring the stock to a boil. Add rice and stir. Reduce heat, cover, and simmer for 20 minutes. Remove from heat.
3. Add cheese, onion, eggs, and butter to the cooked rice in the saucepan and mix well to blend. Gently stir in herbs and milk.
4. Spoon into a 2-quart casserole dish. Bake for 1½ hours.

HERBED POLENTA SLICES

Polenta is cornmeal cooked into a creamy solid about the texture of soft mashed potatoes. It's usually served as a side dish, like potatoes or rice. Also like those starches, it's versatile and can be dressed up or left as plain as you wish. To make polenta, use cornmeal that's about the consistency of sand (a flour-like consistency is too fine). The trick to preparing it is to never stop stirring. Corn is magically associated with prosperity, health, and fertility. These slices are excellent hot, but can also be eaten cold. They're wonderful served with a hearty salad as a main dish. Magical associations of this dish include prosperity, health, and protection.

Serves 8 as a side dish, 4 as a main dish

- 2½ cups chicken or vegetable stock
- ²/₃ cup cornmeal
- ¾ cup grated sharp cheese (such as Gruyère, Swiss, or Emmentaler)
- 3 teaspoons butter, divided
- 1½ teaspoons chopped fresh rosemary
- 1 teaspoon chopped fresh thyme
- 1 teaspoon chopped fresh parsley
- Salt and pepper (optional)
- 8 small sprigs of herbs for garnish (optional)

1. Butter a 9-inch glass pie dish. Preheat oven to 350°F.
2. Bring stock to a boil in a heavy-bottomed pot. Slowly add cornmeal in a stream, stirring constantly with a wooden spoon.
3. Reduce the heat to minimum and keep stirring until the mixture thickens (6–8 minutes). Remove from heat.
4. Add the grated cheese and half the butter. Stir until the cheese has melted and been fully combined with the polenta.
5. Stir in the fresh chopped herbs. Season with salt and/or pepper if desired.
6. Scrape polenta into the buttered baking dish. Spread evenly. Cool until firm (about 30 minutes).
7. Line a baking sheet with foil. Slice the cooled polenta into eight wedges. Remove each wedge from the pie dish to the baking sheet, turning each wedge over so the smooth side is on top. Dot each wedge with a bit of the remaining butter.
8. Bake until heated through (about 10 minutes). In the last 1–2 minutes, add an herbal sprig to the top of each wedge.

Last but certainly not least, here is a recipe for bread. Bread flour is wheat based and, like other grain products, carries the magical association of prosperity. Bread itself represents stability, harmony, and success.

HERB PEASANT BREAD

This recipe is a good base for any combination of herbal additions. Try using fresh herbs, but if you use dry make sure to chop or grind them finely. This bread is wonderful to eat while still warm and spread with lots of butter. Magical associations for this bread are health, prosperity, abundance, and stability.

Makes 1 loaf or round

- 1 tablespoon sugar
- 1 cup warm water (around 110°F), divided
- 2 heaping teaspoons yeast (or 1 package)
- 1 teaspoon salt
- 2 cups flour, plus more for kneading
- 1 tablespoon chopped fresh rosemary
- 1 tablespoon chopped fresh thyme
- 1 tablespoon chopped fresh dill
- 1 tablespoon chopped fresh chives
- 1 tablespoon olive oil, plus more for coating

1. In a cup or small bowl, stir sugar into ¼ cup of warm water. Sprinkle the yeast over it and allow it to proof until foamy (about 5 minutes).
2. In a large bowl, stir salt into the flour. Make a well in the flour and pour the proofed yeast in.
3. Add the herbs and 1 tablespoon olive oil to the flour mixture. Stir to combine all ingredients.

4. Slowly add remaining warm water as you stir to create a firm dough ball. If you add too much water, simply add a bit of flour to compensate.

5. Scrape the sides of the bowl and add the scrapings to the dough ball. Sprinkle the ball and bowl with a bit of flour. Cover with a clean, damp cloth and set to rise in a warm place with no drafts until doubled in size (approximately 1½ hours).

6. Remove dough from bowl and place on a floured surface. Knead for approximately 5 minutes until smooth and elastic. Sprinkle flour onto the kneading surface as necessary so that the dough does not stick.

7. Shape dough into a flattened circle about 1 inch thick or into a loaf-shaped log. Place on baking sheet. Brush the entire top with olive oil and leave to rise to the height you desire. (Placing the dough in a barely warm oven is a good place for it to rise.)

8. Heat oven to 400°F. (If your bread is rising in the oven, remove it carefully and then heat the oven.) Bake the bread for 10 minutes, or until golden brown.

Other herbal blends that would be delicious additions for bread include:

- 2 teaspoons rosemary, 1 teaspoon oregano, and 1 teaspoon thyme
- 1 small onion (peeled and grated) and 2 teaspoons dill
- 1 small onion (peeled and grated) and 1–2 garlic cloves (peeled and minced)

Appendix

The Magical Associations of Natural Items

THESE LISTS OF MAGICAL ASSOCIATIONS, like the other lists in this book, have been assembled over my years of practice and include both my own associations as well as traditional correspondences. Apart from personal experimentation and work, my sources over the years have included such books as Mrs. M. Grieve's *A Modern Herbal*, Scott Cunningham's *Encyclopedia of Magical Herbs*, Paul Beyerl's *The Master Book of Herbalism* and *A Compendium of Herbal Magick*, and Jamie Wood's *The Wicca Herbal*.

ALLSPICE:

prosperity, luck, healing, purification, protection, money

ALMOND:

love, money, healing, wisdom

ANGELICA:

protection, hex breaker, healing, psychic abilities, house blessing, purification

ANISE:

psychic abilities, lust, luck, purification, love

APPLE:

love, healing, peace

ASH:

protection, strength, healing, prosperity

BASIL:

love, trust, abundance, prosperity, courage, discipline, protection, marriage, purification, luck, mental abilities

BAY:

protection, purification, endurance, fidelity, psychic powers, divination, wisdom, strength

BAYBERRY:

abundance, prosperity

BENZOIN:

purification, healing, prosperity

BIRCH:
protection, purification, new beginnings, children

CATNIP:
cats, love, beauty, happiness, tranquility, luck

CEDAR:
healing, purification, protection, prosperity

CHAMOMILE:
purification, healing, soothes anxiety, gently heals bad luck, soothes children

CHICKWEED:
animals, love, fidelity, healing, weight loss

CINNAMON:
healing, love, lust, success, purification, protection, money, psychic awareness

CINQUEFOIL (FIVE-FINGER GRASS):
eloquence, cunning, money, protection, sleep, prophetic dreams, purification, love

CLOVE:
protection, mental abilities, attraction, purification, comfort

CLOVER:
lust, hex breaking, prosperity, purification, love, luck, protection, success, fidelity, comfort

COMFREY (BONESET):
healing, prosperity, protection, travel

CORIANDER:
healing, love, lust

CUMIN:
protection, antitheft, love, fidelity

CYPRESS:
protection, comfort, healing

DAISY:
nature spirits, love, children

DANDELION:
longevity, enhances psychic ability, intuition, spiritual and emotional cleanser

DILL:
protection, love, attraction, money, strength, luck, eases sleep, mental abilities, weight loss

ECHINACEA:
healing

ELDER, ELDERFLOWER:
protection from lightning, beauty, divination, prosperity, purification, house blessing, healing, sleep

ELM:
love, protection

EUCALYPTUS:

protection, healing

EYEBRIGHT:

truth, pierces through illusion, certainty, psychic ability

FENNEL:

courage, strength, cleansing

FEVERFEW:

love, fidelity, protection, healing

FLAX:

money, protection, beauty, healing

GARDENIA:

love, attraction, peace, meditation

GARLIC:

healing, house blessing, protection, lust, antitheft

GERANIUM:

love, healing, protection, fertility

GINGER:

healing, love, money, energy

HAWTHORN:

protection, fertility, happiness

HAZEL:

mental abilities, fertility, protection, wisdom, luck

HEATHER:

protection, rain, luck

HELIOTROPE:

clairvoyance, psychic abilities, health, money

HIBISCUS:

love, lust, divination, harmony, peace

HONEYSUCKLE:

abundance, luck, prosperity, eases sorrow, enhances psychic abilities (do not use the berries; they are poisonous)

HOPS:

healing, sleep

HYACINTH:

love, comfort, protection

HYSSOP:

purification, protection

JASMINE:

love, attraction, prosperity, tranquility

JUNIPER:

cleansing, purification, protection against accidents, protection against illness, love, antitheft, fertility, psychic abilities

LAVENDER:

healing, love, happiness, heals grief and guilt, sleep, tranquility, protection, purification, peace, house blessing, wisdom, children, marriage

LEMON:

purification, love, protection, happiness

LICORICE:

love, lust, protection, fidelity

LILAC:

protection, beauty, love, psychic abilities, purification, prosperity

LILY:

protection, love antidote, truth

LIME:

love, purification, luck, sleep

LOTUS:

blessing, meditation, protection

MAPLE:

sweetness, prosperity, marriage, love, money

MARIGOLD:

positive energy, protection, eases legal stress, increases psychic awareness, peace

MARJORAM:

protection, love, happiness, health, money, marriage, comfort

MEADOWSWEET:

peace, love, happiness, psychic awareness

MINT:
purification, preserves health, clarity of mind, protects travelers, attracts money, health, love, success

MISTLETOE:
healing, protection, love, fertility, sleep, luck

MUGWORT:
divination, protection, healing, strength, lust, psychic power, fertility, protects travelers

NETTLE:
cleansing, protects from danger, protects health

NUTMEG:
clairvoyance, health, luck, fidelity

OAK:
purification, protection, prosperity, health and healing, money, fertility, luck, strength

ONION:
healing, protection, purification

ORANGE:
love, joy, purification, prosperity

OREGANO:
peace

PARSLEY:

healing, lust, fertility, love, passion, protection, hex breaker, prosperity, purification, eases grief

PATCHOULI:

money, fertility, lust, clairvoyance, divination, love, attraction

PEPPER:

protection, purification

PINE:

prosperity, healing, purification, fertility

POPPY:

fertility, abundance, sleep, love

ROSE:

healing, love, conciliation, restoration, self-love, attracts love and good fortune, heals trouble, enhances psychic ability

ROSEMARY:

cleansing, protection, healing, longevity, improves memory and concentration

ROWAN (MOUNTAIN ASH):

purification, house blessing, protection, healing, psychic abilities, wisdom, strengthens spells

RUE:

protection, mental abilities, purification, health, comfort

SAGE:

healing, longevity, good health, psychic awareness, protection

ST. JOHN'S WORT:

courage, power of the sun, fertility, purification, healing, positive energy

TARRAGON:

cleansing, regeneration, transformation

THYME:

purification, psychic cleansing, divination, healing, enhances memory, eases sleep, courage

VALERIAN (ALL-HEAL):

purification, protection, healing, love, sleep, attraction

VANILLA:

love, prosperity, lust, energy, mental abilities, creativity

VERBENA (VERVAIN):

purification, protection, blessings, communication with nature spirits

VIOLET:

tranquility, love, luck, protection, healing

WALNUT:

healing, mental abilities

WILLOW:

communication, eloquence, protection, healing, love, dreams

YARROW:

marriage, courage, love and friendship, psychic abilities, hex breaking

Bibliography

Alden, Lori. *The Cook's Thesaurus.* 1996–2006, www.foodsubs .com.

Andrews, Ted. *Enchantments of the Faerie Realm: Communications with Nature Spirits & Elementals.* St. Paul, MN: Llewellyn, 1993.

Beith, Mary. *Healing Threads: Traditional Medicines of the Highlands and Islands.* Edinburgh: Polygon, 1995.

Beyerl, Paul. *Compendium of Herbal Magick.* Custer, WA: Phoenix Publishing, 1998.

———. *Master Book of Herbalism.* Custer, WA: Phoenix Publishing, 1984.

Compton, Madonna Sophia. *Herbal Gold: Healing Alternatives.* St. Paul, MN: Llewellyn Publications, 2000.

Cowan, Eliot. *Plant Spirit Medicine.* Newberg, OR: Swan, Raven & Company, 1995.

Cunningham, Scott. *Cunningham's Encyclopedia of Crystal, Gem & Metal Magic, 1st ed.* St. Paul, MN: Llewellyn Publications, 1988.

———. *Cunningham's Encyclopedia of Magical Herbs, 2nd ed.* St. Paul, MN: Llewellyn Publications, 2000.

————. *Cunningham's Encyclopedia of Wicca in the Kitchen*, 3rd ed. St. Paul, MN: Llewellyn Publications, 2003.

————. *Earth, Air, Fire, Water: More Techniques of Natural Magic*. St. Paul, MN: Llewellyn Publications, 1991.

————. *Earth Power: Techniques of Natural Magic*. St. Paul, MN: Llewellyn Publications, 1983.

————. *Magical Herbalism: The Secret Craft of the Wise*. St. Paul, MN: Llewellyn Publications, 1983.

Davies, Owen. *Cunning-Folk: Popular Magic in English History*. London: Hambledon and London, 2003.

Dugan, Ellen. *Cottage Witchery: Natural Magick for Hearth and Home*. St. Paul, MN: Llewellyn Publications, 2005.

————. *Garden Witchery: Magick from the Ground Up*. St. Paul, MN: Llewellyn Publications, 2003.

Eason, Cassandra. *Modern-Day Druidess*. New York: Citadel Press, 2003.

Farrar, Janet and Stewart. *The Witches' Goddess: The Feminine Principle of Divinity*. Custer, WA: Phoenix Publishing, 1987.

————. *The Witches' God: Lord of the Dance*. Custer, WA: Phoenix Publishing, 1998.

Green, Marian. *Wild Witchcraft: A Guide to Natural, Herbal and Earth Magic*. (Previously published as *Elements of Natural Magic*.) London: Thorsons, 2002.

————. *A Witch Alone: Thirteen Moons to Master Natural Magic*. London: Thorsons, 1995.

Grieve, Mrs. Maud. *A Modern Herbal in Two Volumes: The Medicinal, Culinary, Cosmetic and Economic Properties, Cultivation and Folk-Lore of Herbs, Grasses, Fungi, Shrubs & Trees with Their Modern Scientific Uses*. (Originally published 1931.) New York: Dover Publications, 1982.

Harner, Michael. *The Way of the Shaman: A Guide to Power and Healing*. New York: Bantam Books, 1982.

Hobbs, Christopher. *Herbal Remedies for Dummies*. Foster City, CA: IDG Books, 1998.

Hoffman, David. *The Complete Illustrated Holistic Herbal: A Safe and Practical Guide to Making and Using Herbal Remedies*. Shaftesbury: Element Books, 1996.

Lipp, Frank J. *Healing Herbs*. London: Duncan Baird Publishers, 1996.

Lust, John. *The Herb Book: The Complete and Authoritative Guide to More Than 500 Herbs*. New York: Beneficial Books, 2001.

McArthur, Margie. *Wisdom of the Elements: The Sacred Wheel of Earth, Air, Fire, and Water*. Freedom, CA: Crossing Press, 1998.

Monaghan, Patricia. *The Book of Goddesses and Heroines, rev. ed.* St. Paul, MN: Llewellyn Publications, 1990.

Morrison, Dorothy. *Bud, Blossom, & Leaf: The Magical Herb Gardener's Handbook*. St. Paul, MN: Llewellyn Publications, 2001.

Moura, Ann. *Green Witchcraft: Folk Magic, Fairy Lore, & Herb Craft*. St. Paul, MN: Llewellyn Publications, 1996.

Müller-Ebeling, Claudia, Christian Rätsch, and Wolf-Dieter Storl. *Witchcraft Medicine: Healing Arts, Shamanic Practices, and Forbidden Plants*. Translated by Annabel Lee. Rochester, VT: Inner Traditions, 2003.

Murphy-Hiscock, Arin. *Power Spellcraft for Life: The Art of Crafting and Casting for Positive Change*. Avon, MA: Provenance Press, 2005.

Palin, Poppy. *Craft of the Wild Witch: Green Spirituality & Natural Enchantment*. St. Paul, MN: Llewellyn Publications, 2004.

RavenWolf, Silver. *American Folk Magic: Charms, Spells, and Herbals.* (Originally published 1995 as *HexCraft.*) St. Paul, MN: Llewellyn Publications, 1998.

Sierralupe, Suzan Stone. "Path of the Green Witch." *SageWoman* (Issue 41, Spring 1998).

The United States National Arboretum: USDA National Plant Hardiness Zone Map, www.usna.usda.gov/Hardzone/index.html. (accessed April 27, 2017).

Valiente, Doreen. *Natural Magic.* Custer, WA: Phoenix Publishing, 1975.

West, Kate. *The Real Witches' Garden: Spells, Herbs, Plants and Magical Spaces Outdoors.* London: Element, 2004.

Williams, Jude C. *Jude's Herbal Home Remedies: Natural Health, Beauty, & Home-Care Secrets.* St. Paul, MN: Llewellyn Publications, 1998.

Index